• HALSGROVE DISCOVER SERIES ➤

NORTHERN IRELAND'S ANCIENT SITES

Diana Dicker

HALSGROVE

First published in Great Britain in 2010

British Library Cataloguing-in-Publication Data
A CIP record for this title is available from the British Library

ISBN 978 1 84114 991 2

HALSGROVE
Halsgrove House,
Ryelands Industrial Estate,
Bagley Road, Wellington, Somerset TA21 9PZ
Tel: 01823 653777   Fax: 01823 216796
email: sales@halsgrove.com

Part of the Halsgrove group of companies
Information on all Halsgrove titles is available at: www.halsgrove.com

Printed and bound in China by Toppan Leefung Printing Ltd

Contents

Introduction   5

Chapter 1. Belfast   20

Chapter 2. The Ards Peninsula
            and Strangford Lough   51

Chapter 3. The Glens of the
            Antrim Coast   62

Chapter 4. The Dramatic North
            Coast   71

Chapter 5. Derry and the
            Plantation Heartland   84

Chapter 6. The Ulster American
            Experience   95

Chapter 7. The Fermanagh
            Waterland   108

Chapter 8. Garden Lands of
            Armagh   120

Chapter 9. The Wilds of the
            Mourne Mountains   135

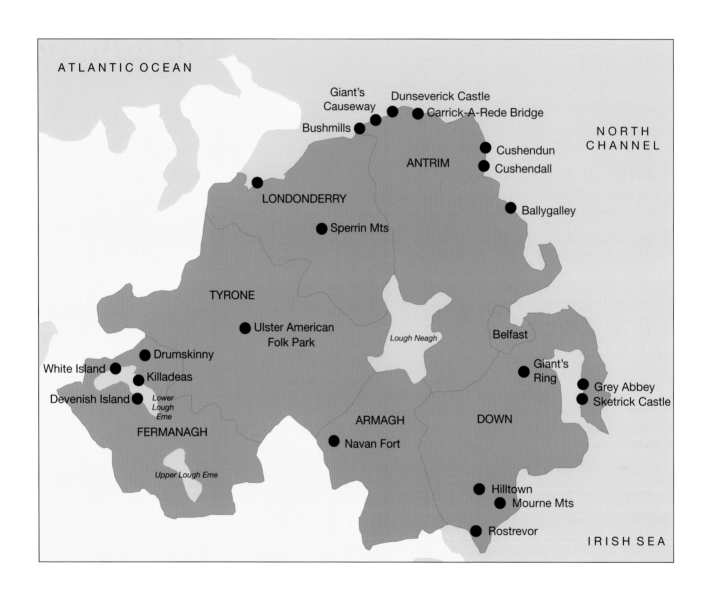

ATLANTIC OCEAN

NORTH CHANNEL

Giant's Causeway
Dunseverick Castle
Carrick-A-Rede Bridge
Bushmills
Cushendun
ANTRIM
Cushendall
LONDONDERRY
Ballygalley
Sperrin Mts
TYRONE
Ulster American Folk Park
Lough Neagh
Belfast
Drumskinny
Giant's Ring
White Island
Grey Abbey
Killadeas
Sketrick Castle
Devenish Island
Lower Lough Eme
DOWN
FERMANAGH
ARMAGH
Navan Fort
Upper Lough Eme
Hilltown
Mourne Mts
Rostrevor
IRISH SEA

Introduction

Northern Ireland oozes history and there are heritage centres and museums of all sizes at every turn. The landscape is swathed in history, hills and valleys are scattered with ancient monuments from the Stone, Bronze and Iron Ages. Towns have signature buildings from the Norman conquerors, medieval times and Plantation eras while cities bear witness to the industry and evolution of Northern Ireland and are ablaze with murals depicting both sides of the conflict from King William crossing the Boyne in 1690 to Celtic Freedom Fighters.

One is always just a stone's throw away from a megalithic monument, from the grand and spectacular Beaghmore stone rows to a small huddle of stones wedged in a housing estate. The folks at 91 Ballylumford Road in Larne are unable to park outside their house as a giant dolmen, known as the Druid's Altar, is in the way.

Driving at sheep speed.

Over the centuries waves of settlers have flooded over to Ulster, which we now know as Northern Ireland, from the Celts who went on to build the great Christian monasteries during the European Dark Ages and the invading Vikings to the Normans and English-Scots. In turn the Scots-Ulster emigrants moved on to open the frontiers of the New World of America.

And now the tourist is the next wave of visitor. And people make them welcome. Locals may be shy to speak; they are not assertively friendly, not exuding exhausting or invasive bonhomie, but are genuinely friendly, helpful, open and often funny, very funny. nonetheless. They are a quiet sort of folk and a rural ethos spreads into the town. But approachable and interesting, nothing is too much trouble. And many wonderful conversations are to be had at the bars, markets and byways across the country as well as at the open doorways of smaller hamlets.

This is life in the slow lane. Cars even drive below the speed limit on motorways. And vehicles stop on zebra crossings before you step on the white lines. Make no plans to get anywhere fast on narrow, curvy country roads slowed by farm vehicles and sheep.

Overview of Carrick-a-Rede rope bridge.

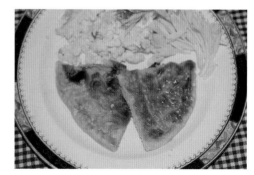

Modern bungalow with rainbow.

Soda farls in packet.

Soda bread on a plate.

Although many elements of the past have gone; the eels of Lough Neagh are no longer caught with hazel wood traps; Carrick-a-Rede is no longer the perilous rope bridge of the salmon fishermen but a very safe structure tended by the National Trust; and the little white stone cottages have been replaced by very ordinary bungalows. But, nevertheless, an ancient cultural heritage is alive and well in the contemporary world.

Convenience stores sell farls, a potato scone or savoury cake, and soda bread. Dulse seaweed and yellowman toffee are seaside treats. And the Ulster breakfast with white and black pudding, a sausage with the black pudding coloured by pigs' blood, and a vat of porridge spiced with a splash of whiskey, honey and cream is a great start to the day. And there is wild salmon or bass caught offshore for supper.

The Irish tongue has died away as a primary language but a tapaleerie (light headed) gebberloon (idiot) might still talk blaffum (nonsense). There are the beginnings of a resurgence of interest in the Gaelic tongue and culture. At every turn there is a tale to be told whether taken from the Ulster Cycle, an epic myth of cattle raids and dynastic struggle, or a local legend. Prayer rags are still tied to trees at holy wells to gain cures and healing traditions run strong with regular pilgrimages to sacred sites such as the healing holy well at St Patrick's, Belcoo.

Religious shrines have been vital for thousands of years from the Celtic Druids 500 BC with chambered cairns and a two-headed god and the pre-Christian myths of magic and fairies to the monastic sites of St Patrick and the early Christians. And legends resound across the centuries such as Maguire's burial yew tree which bleeds every autumn in memory of him being slaughtered by a kinsman on the church's altar in 1484.

There is an imprint of the past on the modern day. The ancient roads of the Celts are still walked. A sophisticated people, the early Celts did not commit to writing but a strong oral tradition brought the sagas of the shape shifting god-kings and the "little people" as well as epics of heroic exploits into the Christian age when the tales and legends were written down, even though the Vikings destroyed the libraries. Although Gaelic tradition was eroded with the Protestant conquest by the English, Calvinists, French Huguenots and Scottish from the seventeenth century, the Victorian interest in folklore recorded many of the legends and myths which thread through contemporary culture today.

HISTORY

As the Ice Age faded from northern Europe some ten thousand years ago a new landscape was unveiled which slowly became inhabited. Nomadic Mesolithic peoples journeyed across the continent, sailing from Scotland in wooden boats, arriving as the first inhabitants of Ireland around 7,500BC. Initially they settled the coastal plains and river banks.

Within three thousand years these hunter-gatherers of the dense forest gave way to settled Neolithic farmers with artistic skills and elaborate rituals. By 2,500BC the Bronze Age people were working with metal. The Irish fashioned iconic, sophisticated gold work. With the dawning of the Iron Age and the emergence of the mining and metalworking Celts the intricate, swirling La Tene patterns and stone dolmens appear.

Around 300BC the great legends, myths and fairy stories evolve amongst the Celtic people known as Gaels with the Druid priesthood. Later the tales are written down by the Christians. These heroic sagas from Cu Chulainn, the semi-divine champion of early Ulster called Ulaid, to Conor, who ruled from Emain Macha now visited at Navan Fort, are still vital today.

Navan Fort: the top of the mound

Red Hand of Ulster. Close-up Ulster Hall.

From across the sea, waves of raiding Vikings challenged the peace for some 300 years until finally being defeated by Brian Boru in 1014.

In the mid twelfth century the Anglo-Normans began to move in. The symbol of Ulster is the red hand which comes from the twelfth century legendary race between the Gaelic MacDonnell and the Norman de Burgh. The first to land on shore would win and rule the land. Seeing that de Burgh was ahead, MacDonnell cut of his hand and threw it ashore to stake his claim.

By the sixteenth century the troops of Queen Elizabeth I were victorious over the defending dominant O'Neill clan bringing the territory firmly under English rule. The Tudor plantations were established spawning the origins of the conflict, now known as The Troubles, which has dogged Northern Ireland to the present day, as native Catholics surrendered lands to incoming Protestants from Scotland and Ireland. The town plan introduced at this time based on a central square, known as the Diamond, with church, courthouse and market square, Celtic crosses, monuments and streets radiating off is still evident in towns and cities across the region today.

By the 1640s the English forces of King Charles I squashed the native Irish bid for power, clearing the land of Catholics and imposing Scottish Protestant plantations in their place. In 1652 Cromwell subdued further insurgence giving Roundhead soldiers Irish land in lieu of wages.

After the restoration of the monarchy, King James II reinstated the position of the Catholics. However, with the crowning of William of Orange, the tide turned and Protestant dominance returned from the 1690s. This is the era of the famous lengthy siege of Protestant Londonderry when the Apprentice Boys closed the city gates against the attack of the Catholic supporters of King James called Jacobites.

In the eighteenth century the Anglo Irish nobility built the grand Georgian stately mansions or "big houses" including Mount Stewart House on the Ards Peninsula and Castle Coole near Enniskillen. The Scots-English descendant landowners continued to live in fortified manor houses.

The Province of Northern Ireland was created after partition in 1921. It is known as Ulster, the name of one of four traditional kingdoms and first to embrace Christianity after St Patrick's arrival in 432AD. The resulting fighting, The Troubles, between the Catholic and Protestant para-military forces largely shaped the image of Northern Ireland in the twentieth century.

Orangeman decorations, Broughshane.

Derry Walls, Ferryquay Gate – the gate the Apprentice Boys closed against the Jacobites.

Plantation Era Gatehouse.

Fortified Manor House – Ballygally Castle.

Antrim Estate Office.

Castlewellan Church – typical dominant Protestant church in the town centre.

The Troubles have caused much grief for the people of Northern Ireland. But on 22 May, 1998, over 70% of the people endorsed the Good Friday Agreement with "partnership, equality and mutual respect." The ceasefire largely holds, albeit a bit shakily at times, as most people unite against violence and strive for peace.

Politics and religion frame the experience of exploring historic sites in Northern Ireland. Yet politics, religion and history make for a potent mix and to avoid trouble, avoid these topics. Do not embark on such conversations flippantly.

History is evident in the town and landscape at every turn whether it is a planned trip to a magnificent monument or tripping over something interesting unexpectedly. In order of age, this is a timeline of monuments that will be encountered while looking at Ulster's rich history.

Worked flint sites such as the raised Curran beach at Larne are littered with thousands of pieces of flint flakes and evidence of the production of flint tools and weapons. Along with the not very visible archaeological evidence of wooden huts and charcoal fires, such as the site at Mountsandel, worked flints are the only traces of the first inhabitants of Ireland, the Mesolithic or Middle Stone Age people, from 10,000 years ago.

Megalithic chambered tombs, the dolmen with a large, flat capstone supported by three or more upright stones like a table or tripod, were created by Neolithic agriculturists, 3,000–2,000BC. Originally covered in a mound of earth they are now bare and the huge stone slab construction is visible. Some dolmen sites have a more complex layout with an entrance passageway and forecourt with an outlining kerb. They are thought to have evolved from a simpler cist barrow burial and are similar to court cairns with an underground room, larger than the dolmen's internal space.

Stone circles and standing stones with ritual usage and astronomical calendar possibilities are the oldest monuments dating from the Neolithic Age and on into the

Dolmen – Tirnony Dolmen, Maghera. Note the domed stone gate post in rear.

Stone Circle, Drumskinny, Fermanagh.

13

Bronze Age. Called stone circles these ceremonial sites are usually not pure circles but are elliptical. They are considered to have astronomical significance with sight lines to the rising or setting sun or moon at solstices. Standing stones known as orthostats are single stones.

Early Bronze Age is evident in very large earthen circles or henges such as Giant's Ring, 2,700BC, at Drumbo, near Belfast. These man-made structures are impractical for defence and are of ritual and religious significance.

Bronze Age ancient site signature is the ring fort known as a rath. The defensive principle of placing a fort safely on top of a hill lasted from the Bronze Age through Norman times with circular ramparts protectively enclosing daub and wattle homesteads and grand wooden royal halls. The steep banks of earth and stones further heightened by a deep external ditch were housing fortifications for the clan head and large connected families along with their livestock. Effective at keeping out wolves, thieves and intruders as well as keeping farm animals in, the rath would not withstand a concerted attack. Hill forts utilise the hill top as a natural defence and many of them had later castles constructed over the rath.

Henge, Giant's Ring, Drumbo.

Crannogs, artificial islands in lakes and marshes, are waterland forts and homesteads constructed from oak stakes driven into the lake, river or marsh bottom then built up with logs, branches, stones and earth with a dwelling or two on top. These defensive farmsteads originated in the late Bronze Age with most dating to the later Iron Age. These artificial circular island dwelling settlements were reached by either causeway or boat and have both a defence and a display of status aspect. And the truncated residue, looking like a small natural island, can still be seen today. An excellent example is at Loughbrickland, near Banbridge.

Early Irish churches, stone churches from after the ninth century are the only architectural remains of the pre-Norman period, fifth to twelfth centuries, when buildings were mostly made of wood and have not survived.

Round towers are slender, stately and emblematic towers which are tall, tapering up to a conical stone roof, monastic belfries with hand-rung alarm bells. The door, reached by a retractable rope ladder, stands defensively some 12 feet (3.5 m) from ground. Both refuge from raiders and watchtower, the round towers stored food and treasure, including manuscripts, during the Viking raids during the ninth to the eleventh centuries. These early medieval stone towers are good signposts to remains of old monastic sites as the door of the tower was opposite the west door of the church.

High crosses are striking carved stones from the eight to the twelfth centuries with biblical or intricate decoration and an iconic circular top. These free standing Celtic Christian crosses from the Early Middle Ages, and later, usually have a ring at the junction of the two arms of the cross. The earlier crosses have geometric motifs but the later decorations are of biblical stories.

Romanesque period churches of the eleventh and twelfth century are identified by chevrons, beading, carved doorways and windows with rounded arches and railings. These monumental churches were the first to have stone rather than wooden roofs supported by thick walls and round arches with large towers and small windows. The stone walls were gaily painted with scenes from daily life as well as the bible and decorated with natural, mythical and pagan images.

Gothic style arrived with the Normans during the thirteenth to sixteenth centuries. Castles evolved from wooden motte and bailey fortifications on the site of rath hill forts to stone buildings. Gothic churches are austere and simple identified by pointed towers and arches with ribbed vaults, flying buttresses and carved cloisters.

Tower houses of the fifteenth century are fortified farms with square tower and walled bawn courtyard. A fine example, Narrow Water Castle near Warrenpoint is strategically placed on the meeting of river and lough. An inhabited defence, the tower house is a residence of a noble family yet can command a strategic site with a very small force of troops.

Bonamargy Church with head of high cross, Ballycastle.

Tower house – tower of Ballygally Castle.

Mass Stones are usually large natural stones, sometimes carved, found in woodland and other secret places. The Penal Laws of 1695 disenfranchised Roman Catholic and Presbyterian Protestants in favour of Church of Ireland adherents with restrictions on land ownership, professions and political power. The laws were aimed to stop Catholic worship and in reaction, congregations created open air places for prayer. The Mass stones were private, natural altars for clandestine religious services. The laws were repealed in 1820.

Georgian architecture from the eighteenth century is evident throughout Northern Ireland from the grand, calm and dignified "big house" rural mansions through the smooth symmetry of the Moravian village of Gracehill outside Ballymena or provincial elegance of small settlements such as Glenarm on the Antrim coast as well as the Belfast townhouse. The Georgian period is defined as the era ruled by the first four Hanovererian kings, all called George, from 1713 through 1840. The elegant townhouse with terraces of regular design and the signature detailed doorway and panelled door as well as the great Palladian houses in an Arcadian landscape define this style inspired by the buildings of ancient Rome and Greece. Castle Coole in County Fermanagh epitomises the calm, smooth and serene Georgian design with a central block plus portico flanked by side wings and all in dignified, icy Portland stone, imported at great cost. The elegance of the era is enjoyed as the last glory before the onslaught of the "satanic mills" of the Industrial Revolution.

Georgian townhouses – downtown Belfast.

Victorian prosperity of industrialisation and the British Empire brought grand edifices, statues and public buildings that are the signature façades of Belfast and the seaside resorts of the north coast and the Ards Peninsula.

Most historic sites in Northern Ireland are open to the public but check ahead as opening times may vary and many sites are on private land with most, except some private residences, available to view by arrangement. As many megalithic sites are on functioning farmland visitors are asked to respect the Country Code closing gates, keeping dogs on leads and similar respect for a working agricultural environment.

Eighteenth century church.

St Malarky Catholic Church, Belfast.

Belfast Telegraph newspaper clock.

WALKING

Whereas checking off the list of "must sees" will need wheels, to truly experience the real Northern Ireland a pair of stout and comfy walking boots is best. Whether it is dramatic hill-walking tramps through the rugged Mourne Mountains or wandering the quiet and empty back roads, once off the beaten track and away from the well trod tourist circuit a ramble is your own unique adventure.

Sharing the life of friendly local people, tales tall and otherwise come alive. And if the head is full of the myths, tales and legends of yore, then the feet have to be in strong shoes, if not wellington boots. Dress for changeable weather and carry waterproofs. Be ready for rainbows. The intense colour of the landscape is painted by rain, a soft rain filtered with sunshine. And beware of the bogs.

To walk safely a good map is recommended. Many trailheads are marked but signposts wither along the path. The Ulster Way is 560 miles of, mostly, marked trails encircling Northern Ireland along stunning coastline, rural scenery and forest paths and also interconnecting with other trails.

Rainbow.

Giant's Causeway.

Take a good map. Sign posts on the trail wither along the way. The trail appears to lead to a field with bull in it.

CHAPTER 1

Belfast

Mural, Belfast. This shows unity and peace.

Ancient sites are thin on the ground in Belfast as the city, unlike rural Ulster, bore the brunt of the burgeoning Industrial Revolution, although there are excellent historic, and prehistoric, resources in museums and libraries. There is evidence of early occupation of the area since Mesolithic times with the first written mention being in 668, the Vikings dragged their long boats over the sandbanks in 900 and the Normans arrived in 1177. Belfast was of scant importance, except as a crossing of the River Lagan. Largely overshadowed by Carrickfergus, the administrative centre up the coast, Belfast began to develop in the mid-eighteenth century being officially declared a city by Queen Victoria in 1888. During the nineteenth century the city and seaport dramatically expanded founded initially on traditional spinning and weaving then fuelled by the growth of linen mills and exploding industrialisation.

Sitting at the centre of an encircling saucer of hills, Belfast is the political capital of Northern Ireland. The names Ulster and Northern Ireland are often interchangeable for this geo-political area defined on 22 June 1921. Ulster was one of the four ancient provinces from Celtic times and the original Ulster included two counties which are now part of the Republic of Ireland. The remaining six counties were those dominated by the descendants of Protestant plantation settlers in the 1600s that today make Northern Ireland, administered from Stormont in Belfast.

Ringed by hills, one can always look up and see green peaks. Fronted by a lough, Belfast evolved from a small settlement that, four hundred years ago, was called Beal Feirst which translates as "the mouth of the sandy ford." Little had changed since the Anglo-Normans built a castle here in 1177. Then the town began to grow with the development of the local linen industry after James I installed the English Sir Arthur Chichester to govern the area. The organisational skills and work ethic of the Protestant French Huguenots who arrived later in the seventeenth century boosted development setting the stage for the Industrial Revolution.

A modern city, Belfast has a cultural heritage that stretches back linking past centuries with contemporary communities. The dramatic political murals along both the Protestant Shankill Road and Catholic Falls Road created in the second half of the twentieth century have images relating to historical events going back to the sixteenth century and beyond. They can be seen with Coiste Irish Political Tours, walking tours led by political ex-prisoners. Ancient grievances that had smouldered in the minority Catholic population festered, erupting in civil protest in the late 1960s that undermined social harmony through the end of the twentieth century.

Since the blossoming peace process launched with the Easter Agreement, Belfast has reinvented itself as a cultural centre with major refurbishment of the historic City Hall, restoration of classic concert venue Ulster Hall, as well as the rebuilding of Ulster Museum. There is a resurgence of the Gaelic language. The publican at Kelly's Cellars, Belfast's oldest pub founded in 1720, is a Gaelic speaker and there are appropriate drinking sayings such as "when drink is in, whit is out" written in Gaelic on the walls.

Ulster Hall – Musicians play outside.

Ulster Hall.

Lily the landlady at Kelly's Cellars is a Gaelic speaker and has Gaelic sayings written on the walls, see above fireplace.

Above: *Kelly's Cellars. Belfast.*

Left: *Kelly's Cellars with St Mary's church in the background.*

The city is divided into four quarters: The Bohemian Queen's Quarter is home to the University and the Botanical Gardens with the 1829 Palm House, one of the earliest curved glass and iron structures in the world; the oldest is the Cathedral Quarter with the Cathedral Church of St Anne with two marbled floor paths, one leads to sin and the other virtue – the former leads nowhere, the second heads straight to the sanctuary, at its heart; the newest is the Gaeltacht Quarter promoting and presenting the Irish language and culture; and the Titanic Quarter is founded on the shipyard heritage.

Little narrow alleys called "entries" house some long established pubs including White's Tavern, associated with the wine trade since 1630, in Winecellar Entry. Originally a wholesalers in the vintners' area, the pub has thick heavy beams that were strong enough to store barrels upstairs and big doors to roll the barrels in and out. The Morning Star in Pottinger's Entry is one of the last of the traditional oyster houses. It was here that the Presbyterian leader Henry Joy McCracken was brought after his execution in 1798. His sister Mary Ann McCracken had bribed the hangman and she had hoped to revive him.

St Anne's Cathedral – Cathedral Quarter.

Ferry coming into port – Shipyard/Titanic Quarter.

Pottinger's Entry.

The heavy beams of White's Tavern.

Morning Star – Mary Ann McCracken brought her hanged brother here.

VICTORIAN AND EDWARDIAN BELFAST

Belfast is at the core of Northern Ireland's triumphant Victorian Industrial Revolution. Self-confident, monumental public buildings and statuary are a testament to the Victorian financial boom and glory of the Empire such as the spectacularly ornate and ostentatious City Hall, the fantastically evocative Grand Opera House and majestic Italianate stucco Ulster Hall as well as the leaning tower memorial for Prince Albert. Two mammoth cranes named Samson and Goliath watch over the city from the Harland & Wolff shipyard, builders of the RMS *Titanic* and a witness to a once great ship building heritage.

At the centre of the city is Donegall Square, a testament to prosperity, with the opulent and imposing Edwardian City Hall at its heart with a petticoat of statues and monuments to the Empire including Queen Victoria and the *Titanic* Memorial. Nearby is a wedding-cake architectural fantasy, the very pink St Malachy's church built in 1844 with dramatic

City Hall.

The Opera House.

fan-vaulted ceilings and octagonal turrets with arrow slits, the bell tower was removed as the ringing disturbed the whiskey maturation at the neighbouring distillery.

To the west, two other architectural wonders of imagination and fantasy lie cheek by jowl and both are restored to their former decadent and lavish splendour. The Grand Opera House of 1894 is all exotic and sumptuous opulence of gilt and red plush with an Oriental theme and opposite is a glitzy gin-palace with a façade of glittering tiles. The Crown Liquor Saloon is a dizzying display of Victorian extravaganza with scrolled ceiling, little wooden snugs with carved heraldic beasts for a quiet drink of Guinness, an exuberantly tiled bar and all still lit with the soft and flattering glow of gas lights.

Crown Liquor Saloon – interior.

Crown Liquor Saloon – exterior.

GEORGIAN BELFAST

In contrast to the flamboyance of Victorian Belfast, Clifton House is a dignified and elegant Georgian building of 1744 that is an indicator of the restrained stylish grace of eighteenth century Belfast. Ironically, it was constructed as the Poor House originally known as the Charitable Institute for the Aged and Infirm. Grand balls were held to raise funds to support the institution which still functions as an event venue today. Topped by an octagonal spire flanked by redbrick wings, Clifton House is clearly visible from the street. It has been converted into private accommodation but there are opportunities to see inside the core heritage area by appointment.

Clifton House and concern for those in need and social injustice is indicative of the Enlightenment liberalism of the Presbyterian merchants whose wealth was founded on linen. During the Society of United Irishmen rebellion Clifton House was considered to be housing supporters of the cause. After Henry Joy McCracken was hanged in 1798 the military, then housed next door to Clifton House, commanded the rebel leader's uncles, editors of the family-owned *News Letter* newspaper, to clear the Poor House in 48 hours.

*Belfast Charitable Society –
Clifton House.*

His sister, the feminist and muslin manufacturing entrepreneur Mary Ann McCracken, had tried in vain to save her brother from the hangman, and spent her life campaigning for social justice and political freedom while tending to the welfare of Clifton House's needy residents.

Librarians have been lending books from the Linen Hall Library since 1788. The city's oldest library is home to an extensive and renowned collection of Irish material, rare books including early printed works and a political collection explored through a warren of wooden cases filled with small index cards. Visiting readers are welcome to browse and stop for a coffee in the Reading Room café. This atmospheric library with an impressive brass railed stone staircase was founded by the Belfast Society for Promoting Knowledge and is now housed in an old stone and brick linen warehouse.

Along Joy Street and around the block in Hamilton Street are the last of the remaining Georgian townhouses from the city centre. Originally merchants' houses, the redbrick row later became lodgings for theatricals for nearby music halls. On the waterfront, McHugh's Bar lays claim to being the city's oldest building. Constructed in 1711, its proximity to the docks made it more bordello than bar but is suitably tamed today.

Linen Hall Libray.

Linen Hall Library, interior.

Joy Street – last Georgian houses in Central Belfast.

McHughes – reputedly the city's oldest building.

Wedged behind busy shopping streets in Rosemary Street is the First Presbyterian Church, a site of worship since the 1690s. The current elliptical church was completed in the late eighteenth century making it the city's oldest surviving place of worship. With a wheel of plasterwork on the oval ceiling, a curved gallery on wooden Corinthian columns and a boat-like bulge of enclosed box pews the church has a peaceful atmosphere. Wesley preached from the majestic wooden pulpit and the Harland family, of shipyard fame, sat in pew number 57.

Similarly tucked away just off the busy thoroughfare of a modern shopping centre is Belfast's first Roman Catholic church. The elegant St Mary's was built in 1784 a result of ecumenical endeavour as the congregations from both the Presbyterian Church and the Church of Ireland helped establish St Mary's.

Knockbreda parish church is a rural Georgian church that has been engulfed by the swirl of suburban Belfast south of the Botanical Gardens. But, perched at the top of a small hill with a 360° sweeping skirt of descending headstones, the churchyard has an atmosphere of country quiet. The church has a simple reaching spire, a welcoming flight of steps to an architecturally iconic Georgian door and an overall elegance bordering on austerity. But immediately behind the church are a collection of splendid, large and majestic eighteenth century mausoleums that rival the grandiosity of ancient dolmen. The church was consecrated in 1737 and the princes of trade and bastions of the Indian army are buried here in great pomp including the merchant Waddell Cunningham who made his fortune in the West Indian slave trade. The Follies Trust is helping to keep the

Interior of First Presbyterian Church in Rosemary Street.

Entrance to First Presbyterian Church in Rosemary Street.

St Mary's Catholic church – the first RC church built with help from both Protestant communities.

Knochbreda church – typical Georgian doorway.

structures standing. Knockbreda continued being a prestige interment site and the names of many of Belfast's great and good can be found on the graves including Sir Charles Lanyon, the Victorian architect whose design has largely shaped central Belfast today including the University, Palm House and Castle.

EARLY CHRISTIAN, MEDIEVAL AND PLANTATION BELFAST

The Anglo Normans built a defensive castle in 1177 at a small but strategic river crossing. Little changed until in 1603 when a small community was founded by the English based on home produced linen manufacture. The linen industry was organised and developed later in the century by the French Huguenots, laying the foundation for the city we now call Belfast. It was English adventurer Sir Arthur Chichester who founded what we recognise as the modern city in 1606 filling the new town with Scots Dissenter tradesmen.

Georgian Mausoleum, Knockbreda.

Mausoleum, Knockbreda parish church.

Friar's Bush Graveyard.

Friar's Bush Graveyard – note circular-headed Celtic cross gravestone.

Friar's Bush Graveyard lies cheek by jowl with the rejuvenated Ulster Museum and is considered to be one of the oldest Christian cemeteries in Ireland dating back to the fourteenth century when this was a heavily wooded area.

In the Penal Times during which Catholics were deprived of power, profession and land, the secreted site, now in the heart of urban bustle, hosted clandestine mass in the shade of a thorn tree with an officiating friar smuggled across the river. Once the site of a medieval ecclesiastical community, the walled graveyard was a place of Catholic worship until the establishment of St Mary's in central Belfast. A grassy mound, known as Plaguey Hill, is still a visual reminder of mass burials from plague and the names of many famous figures are inscribed on the headstones in the leafy but locked cemetery. Tours on Sunday relate tales of Victorian medical grave robbers called the "Resurrection Men" and suggestions of pre-history origins.

Below left: *St Matthew's church – Shankill Road, architecturally inspired by old round tower style.*

Below right: *Bullaun Stone at St Matthew's.*

ANCIENT BELFAST

Although Belfast was a thriving area in Megalithic and Neolithic times the evidence has largely been hidden during the centuries, covered over by layers of urban development. However, there are two opportunities to experience ancient Belfast within the city as well as the walk up Cave Hill to the north or a trip out to Giant's Ring in the south.

A short step from central Belfast is the newly rebuilt Ulster Museum with a splendid display of treasure from the wrecked Spanish Armada galleon *Girona*. In the grounds is a four-chambered tomb with a shallow forecourt, an area in front of the tomb used for burial rituals; with four orthostats, individual stones that are part of a larger structure; with a cairn, a mound of stones; and a kerb, the enclosing ring of stones. The court-tomb originally came from Ballintaggart in County Armagh and has been moved to and reconstructed at the museum and bears the name of its previous home.

Up the Shankill Road near Woodvale Park, on a plinth outside the architecturally interesting, brick-built St Matthew's church with a modern architectural nod to older ecclesiastical design and round towers, is a bullaun stone dug up from the nearby graveyard. Bullaun stones and their use is a bit of a mystery. Originating in megalithic times these stones with a deep, cup-like, spherical depression are often found alongside ancient churches and monasteries and are considered a pagan ritual element that transmuted to be included in Christian ceremonies.

A DAY OUT

Take a day out, or at least a few hours away, from the hustle and bustle of buzzy Belfast and hop on a train or bus or jump into your car and head up the coast passing Cave Hill and the imposing War Memorial on a bluff above Greenisland.

Below left: *Carrickfergus – a day out from Belfast.*

Below right: *War Memorial at Greensiland.*

DISTANCE: Circular 4.5 miles.

ALLOW: 2 hours.

DIFFICULTY: Moderate-strenuous with steep climb on unsurfaced path through woods, moorland, heath and meadows.

FACILITIES: Refreshments and toilets at Belfast Castle.

TRANSPORT: Buses run to Belfast Castle.

On the outskirts of the city is Cave Hill, 1200 feet (370m). This geographical landmark towers over the city dominating the northern skyline and is seldom out of view. Local people say the shape of the hill inspired Irish writer Jonathan Swift and the silhouette does look like Gulliver's head while tied down on the Lilliputian's beach. The human-like profile has also inspired the hill's nickname of "Napoleon's Nose" mocking the 1798 rebellion inspired by the French Revolution; Napoleon's support was enlisted to help drive the English out of Ireland. Formerly called Beann Mheadagain, hill of Madigan, the name Ben Madigan appears on public buildings and spaces such as local schools, streets and community centres in the area.

Climbing to the summit splendid city views and lough vistas unfurl. The slopes are speckled with Iron Age forts. In ancient times the hill was mined for flint used in tool and weapon production. And in the eighteenth century townsfolk flocked to Cave Hill for the Easter Monday fete at a spring called Volunteers' Well.

The walk starts from the car park at the imposing nineteenth century Scottish Baronial-style Belfast Castle reminiscent of Balmoral and the Scottish Highlands.

Follow the green arrow route from the interpretation board just before the castle entrance. Taking the path on the left, climb to first junction and turn right through woodland. Keep to the left at all junctions until the path breaks free of the tree cover and onto an open plateau.

Take the next path on the left skirting around the Devil's Punchbowl, the remains of a Celtic cattle corral. Pass below the largest of three man-made caves reputedly mined for iron ore and later used for food storage and safe refuge during attack. During the eighteenth century they hosted clandestine meetings to plan the Rebellion and United Irishmen leader Henry Joy McCracken was captured here in 1798 while waiting to escape to America.

The path winds to the right, steadily climbing uphill. Continue on up the steps to the cattle grid in a fence, then follow the grassy path on the left up to the top of the hill, once the O'Neill coronation site on a now destroyed stone "giant's" stone crowning chair, and McArt's Fort. This old rath ring fort has the natural protection of a precipice on one side and encircling defensive ditches around the remaining perimeter and is named for chieftain Eochaid MacArdgal, slain in battle in 1003.

Rejoin the main path and take the gradual descent down the slopes of Cave Hill. Take the lane on the left past the top of Carr's Glen continuing to Upper Cavehill Road. Go down the footpath for a short way before following the path to the left climbing over

the ridge. Return to Belfast Castle along the footpath through the 200-acre estate.

There are eight waymarked trails with shorter and easier walks signed on the lower slopes in the Country Park – route maps are available from the castle.

ANOTHER WALK

A towpath runs from the Belfast Boat Club at Stranmills, south of the Botanical Gardens, and heads out to Moore's Bridge some ten miles later. This is an excellent opportunity to stretch your legs on a well surfaced waterside, rural footpath which is easily accessible to wheelchair users and push chairs as well as city shoes. Go as far as you want, there is an excellent teahouse about two miles out, and turn back when ready.

CARRICKFERGUS – A DAY TRIP OUT OF BELFAST

Reaching out into the ocean, anchored on a spit of dark rocky promontory is the striking and romantic Carrickfergus Castle. This massive and menacing fortress was constructed by conquering Norman military leader John de Courcy in 1180 to guard the entrance to Belfast Lough. A show of strength, this was the main Norman stronghold in the north of Ireland and the seat of power for the Earls of Ulster. Carrickfergus Castle was in use as a military fortification overlooking a busy, strategic sea port until 1928. Well preserved, this is a superior example of a Norman castle in Northern Ireland.

This is the very best opportunity for castle explorations with safe clambering opportunities for children and indoor exhibits to shelter from any inclement briskness while discovering 800 years of castle history. The original portcullis is still in place and ever so slightly cheesy life-sized and costumed models with appropriate weaponry from the different eras dot the ramparts, the four-storey tower and lurk surprisingly in dark corners of dungeons and cellars.

The castle is named for a legendary Dalriadic king whose coronation stone is reputed to be the famous Stone of Scone. Renowned privateer John Paul Jones, father of the American navy, sought, fought and won a battle with British Royal Navy sloop of war HMS *Drake* offshore in 1778. And it was here that King William landed in 1690 on his way to the Battle of the Boyne where he defeated James II, his uncle and father-in-law. There is a colourful Ould Lammas Fair celebration on the last weekend of August.

Named for King Fergus who was shipwrecked off this rocky spur in 320, the town of Carrickfergus is worth a wander. Pass through the arched gateways of the town walls constructed in the early 1600s to defend this settlement, then the primary administrative centre for the whole of the north of Ireland. Carrickfergus overshadowed Belfast in power and importance through to the eighteenth century. The parish church of St Nicholas originated in 1182 and was rebuilt in 1614 and has an interesting leper hole where the infected could take communion from outside the church and an impressive sixteenth century Flemish stained glass window depicting John the Baptist. Poet Louis MacNeice, whose father was rector here from 1907 to 1963, writes of the wonky, skewed and crooked aisle "the church in the form of a cross denoting the list of Christ on the cross in the angle of the nave." At the other end of the market place is the stately Georgian Town Hall. Erected as a courthouse, the sunshine yellow building has also been used as a barracks and hospital and has a museum around the corner.

Opposite: *Carrickfergus Castle.*

Carrickfergus Castle.

45

Carrickfergus Castle – showing the promenade. You have to walk along here to Jackson Centre.

Carrickfergus Castle with life-size figures in period military costume and canon.

A "wee step" out of town, a good half hour hike along the promenade and beyond, is the Andrew Jackson Cottage at Boneybefore. This traditional, single-range, thatched Ulster-Scots cottage farmhouse built in the 1750s is not actually the ancestral home of Andrew Jackson, the 7th President of the United States of America – that was up the road and demolished to make way for the railway. A blue plaque on a stone plinth marks the spot. However, this cottage that was a private residence through the 1970s has been restored with iron pots and griddle on an open fireplace overhung by a daub and wattle canopy and hanging crane, a crockery laden dresser and a collection of traditional Ulster patchwork quilts in the bedrooms. There is an exhibition about the President whose parents emigrated from here in 1765. Call ahead and make an appointment to guarantee entry or peer through the windows.

Celebration of William of Orange, Donaghadee.

In the back garden is the US Rangers Centre, a small museum dedicated to the men of the famous First Battalion combat unit of the elite American Army Unit. The US Rangers were created here in 1942.

On route take a moment to enjoy the Shiels' House, an elegant row of stone homes with shiny red doors founded as a charity to house the homeless during the Great Famine in the 1840s. Although private residences, a bow-shaped entry with an information board gives viewing access.

Above: *Gateway to the town of Carrickfergus.*

Below: *Andrew Jackson Cottage –
white wall, black thatch.*

Carrickfergus's yellow Georgian Town Hall.

If there is time to spare, continue on up the coast to Whitehead, a Victorian railway town and home to the Railway Preservation Society of Ireland. The station houses a plethora of steam train memorabilia, engines and rolling stock as well as a café to enjoy them at leisure. And it is the storage depot for the locomotives and carriages with train trips scheduled during the summer. Before its development in the seventeenth and eighteenth centuries, Whitehead was a small village called Chichester and there are still the modest remains of Castle Chichester. A popular Edwardian resort, there is a coastal walk from the town past Port Davy to Blackhead with the reward of a challenging clamber up the stone steps of the lighthouse.

Divert to Island Magee, an appendix of land that curves to the east of the coast, and take the Ballylumford Road to the Ballylumford Dolmen. Known locally as the "Druid's Altar" this large dolmen has four upright stones with a heavy cap stone and another fallen stone within the structure which may have closed or blocked the entrance to the tomb's chamber. As it is, the entire dolmen blocks the entrance to No. 91 Ballylumford Road whose residents are unable to park outside their house as this large stone remnant of a passage grave is in their front garden.

Returning back along the finger of Island Magee to the mainland, carry on up the coast to the port town of Larne. This was the first part of Ireland to be inhabited, and thousands of Mesolithic and Neolithic flint flakes, arrowheads and scrapers have been uncovered here. It is still the first place of entry for many visitors as it houses the ferry terminal. Many Bostonians can trace their roots to Larne which launched emigration in 1717. At the end of Curran Point, a long spit of gravel to the south of Larne and a primary site for prehistoric worked flint remains, are the ruins of thirteenth-century Olderfleet Castle with Viking foundations but is now overshadowed by an industrial site.

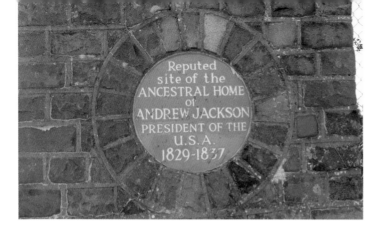

Plaque of Andrew Jackson at Bonneybefore.

Interior Andrew Jackson Cottage.

Above: *Shiels' Houses.*

Left: *Thatching with reeds at Andrew Jackson Cottage with US Rangers Centre to right.*

Ferry into Larne.

OTHER TRIPS

Belfast is the main transport hub with trains, buses and arterial roads stretching out in all directions.

Lisburn, some ten miles to the southwest, is the third largest city of Northern Ireland and its name has evolved from the Gaelic for "fort of the gamblers." It still has the original street plan as laid down in the 1620s. The birthplace of the linen industry, it has a worthy display of early linen production with working handloom linen weavers in the Irish Linen Centre housed in the eighteenth-century Assembly Rooms in the old Market Square.

To the northwest is the modern city of Antrim on the banks of Lough Neagh. It was here that St Patrick was a boy slave before going to France to return in 432 as a missionary. About a mile from town there is the almost perfect 93 feet high ninth century round tower and the Witches Stone prehistoric monument. Great fishing is available at the Shane's Castle estate, family seat of the O'Neills. More information can be obtained from the eighteenth-century Old Market House that has been recently renovated and turned into a tourist centre.

Closer and to the east is Bangor, once a Victorian holiday seaside resort and now a desirable commuter town. Completed in 1637 after the town was granted status as a port in 1620, the Old Custom House is one of the oldest buildings in Ireland to be in continual use. In its heyday it was an important source of revenue for the state. John Simpson, ship's surgeon of the *Titanic*, has a memorial in the graveyard at Bangor Abbey. The original abbey was of such importance that it is one of only four places in Ireland to be mentioned in the Hereford *Mappa Mundi* of 1300.

Down the road on the waterside of Groomsport Harbour is a row of neat, white-washed eighteenth century cottages. Cockle Row cottages are the remaining survivors of traditional fishermen's homes.

CHAPTER 2

The Ards Peninsula and Strangford Lough

Strangfold Lough is a substantial body of water running parallel to the coast south of Belfast and opening out to the sea at Portaferry where some four hundred million tons of tidal water rush through the narrow gap twice a day. The traditional black-sailed Galway Hookers, a distinctive and graceful sailing boat with a hull black from pitch and reddish-brown sails on a single mast, are sometimes seen sailing now for fun rather than the previous commerce such as fishing or carrying peat and other cargo. There is a resurgence of sporting interest in this dramatic sailing boat that handles the rough seas and shallow water of the coastal waters. Their beauty inspires many an artist.

ARDS PENINSULA

Wrapping like an appendix down the eastern side of the lough, the Ards Peninsula is reputed to have the best weather in Ulster. This narrow finger of land has two very different faces. The ocean side to the east is blustery and salty. The loughside to the west is quiet and peaceful. And only a few miles lie between the two.

DONAGHADEE

I've never gone to Donaghadee
That vogue far townlet by the sea;
In Donaghadee I shall never be;
Then why do I sing of Donaghadee?
　　　'Doggerel' by Thomas Hardy.

The treacherous reefs and rocks off this coast have claimed many a ship. Yet Donaghadee is a safe harbour and for many years was the arrival port for the shortest crossing from Portpatrick in Scotland. With the advent of steam, the needs of larger ships saw the transfer of the ferry terminal to Larne in 1849.

But many a famous person landed here in Donaghadee's heyday from poets John Keats and William Wordsworth to writers James Boswell and Daniel Defoe. Russia's Peter the Great passed through as did Franz Liszt along with his piano. And they all called in to the pub now called Grace Neill's. Founded in 1611 as the Kings Arms, the pub now bears the name of a long-time Victorian landlady and a great character who welcomed guests with a big kiss while puffing daylong on her long-stemmed clay pipe. Grace was given the pub by her grandfather and her photograph hangs on the wall today. They say her ghost walks the saloon by night.

Behind the town and overlooking the harbour, with dulse gatherers collecting the edible seaweed from the rocks at low tide, is a prehistoric mound, the Rath. At its summit is the castle-like Moat which was a store for explosives with a fine view to the elegant lighthouse much admired and painted by artists.

Grace Neill's Pub.

Up the coast is the Old Customs House, a 1637 towerhouse and adjoining tower, on the seafront at Bangor. This seventeenth-century defensive structure guarded a seafaring heritage and the state's taxable income from the port. Over the past centuries the building has been in continuous use including being a private residence, a seawater bath house and now the tourist information office.

Bangor Abbey was founded in 558 by Saint Comgall. After alternating waves of destruction and rebuilding, the current abbey presents a primarily Georgian building with a sixteenth-century tower and an octagonal steeple constructed in 1693. There are remnants of a twelfth-century wall nearby. The churchyard has many old and interesting headstones including a *Titanic* memorial.

Across the peninsular on the calmer loughside is the eighteenth-century Mount Stewart, a National Trust-run house and demesne with an award-winning exotic garden planted in the 1920s. This neo-classical mansion was a magnet for important political and social figures from its construction and has on display the twenty-two chairs used at the Congress of Vienna which defined the borders of European countries after the fall of Napoleon.

GREY ABBEY

Also on the quiet loughside is Grey Abbey, a medieval Cistercian monastery. Grey Abbey was founded in 1193 by Affreca, wife of Norman lord John de Courcy, as thanks for being delivered from a storm while visiting her father, the king of the Isle of Man. Today the crumbling ruins nestle into generous park lands at the edge of the village. The traditional medieval physick garden, the apothecary monks' planting of medicinal herbs, has been recreated in the shadow of the pointed Gothic lancet windows. Follow the abbey walls around to find an interesting carved west door.

Heading south towards Portaferry and the ferry crossing that inspires the village's name it is worth a side trip to Kearney, a restored fishing village, before sailing across the "Narrows" to Strangford and the western, land side of Strangford Lough. From midstream, weather permitting, five castles can be seen. There are three megalithic sites in the area: a passage tomb at Millin Way on the peninsula; and over on the mainland a stone burial circle at Ballynoe. A stone circle on Castlemahon Mountain has revealed evidence of fierce fires from the distant past including the burnt bones of a baby.

The Moat on the Rath, Donaghadee.

THE EASTERN SHORES OF STRANGFORD LOUGH

First up on the Strangford side of Strangford Lough is Castle Ward, built by the first Lord Bangor in 1765 in the demesne that was home to the Ward family since the sixteenth century. He wanted the castle constructed in the classical style but his wife, Lady Bangor, preferred the Gothic look. Both got their way but predictably, the marriage did not last long after the mansion's completion. This quirky Jekyll and Hyde "big house" has a serene classical entrance to the house and on the other side, facing the lough, is an ornate Gothic façade. This style dichotomy is reflected in the interior and the gardens and estate have many enchanting features.

Strangford Lough.

DOWNPATRICK

Downpatrick is a pretty town of gaily painted Georgian houses which lays claim, along with the Catholic cathedral in Armagh, to have the grave of St Patrick. However it is generally considered that the cemetery of the Church of Ireland in Downpatrick is the final resting place of the saint and founding father of Christianity in Ireland. The cathedral is constructed on the foundations of an earlier Benedictine Monastery of 1183. The eighteenth century gaol is now a museum and excellent resource for information on St Patrick, the St Patrick's Way passes up, through and around the area.

St Patrick was swept ashore in 432 during high seas at Strangford Lough on route to Antrim where he had tended his flocks of sheep or pigs for six years while a young slave. He began his mission to convert the Celts to Christianity from the rolling hills of Saul, just down the road from Downpatrick. Pilgrims and visitors alike can follow in his footsteps on the St Patrick's Trail locally including the mountain-top pilgrimage site on the summit of Slieve Patrick, the ruins of St Tassach's church at Rahlop where he was given the last rites and holy wells at Struell.

The Saint Patrick's Trail is a linear drive of over 92 miles linking fifteen Christian sites primarily in the Downpatrick and Armagh areas that have a connection with the patron saint, his mission and legacy. The trail starts at the North Down Museum, a small Christian heritage centre with early manuscripts and a ninth-century monk's hand bell, in Bangor. From Bangor Abbey the trail continues to Grey Abbey, Saul Church and Down Cathedral before carrying on to St Tassach's church, Struell Wells and Inch Abbey. In contrast to the nearby Georgian Down County Museum the Saint Patrick's Centre is a custom built interactive exhibition hall using high tech to retell ancient tales.

On the edge of town is Inch Abbey, a ruined Cistercian Abbey constructed in 1189 by the Norman John de Courcy as an act of repentance for his destruction of another abbey nearby. The remains of this large monastic site include an impressive east window, priest sedilla seats and a piscine for washing altar vessels. The wealthy monastery was constructed over an earlier pre-Norman Celtic religious site built on, what at the time was, an island in the Quoile marshes.

From the twelfth to fifteenth centuries sailor monks from Inch and sister abbeys ferried grain, fish and salt over to beleaguered abbeys in England. Using the sun and stars to navigate, the 60-oar galleys brought stone and iron ore back to Ireland.

Founded in 1642, Denvirs Hotel has many original features including stone floors, an inglenook fireplace and a bar crafted from wood reclaimed from wrecked ships. And it was a member of the original hotel family that went to America and founded a small settlement in Colorado known today as Denver.

Nearby is the well preserved Kilclief Castle. This stately, grey, stone early tower house was built in 1440 for the Bishop of Down and has stunning square turrets and spiral staircase. At loughside Killyleagh a nineteenth century castle built on thirteenth century foundations dominates the village with fantasy Disneyland-style turrets. Although a private home, the gates are usually left open for visitors to take a peak.

Down on the coast is Ardlass, a fishing village with the ruined, four-storey Jordan's castle, a tower house built for a successful fifteenth century merchant at its centre. Around the bay is Killough, an eighteenth century grain and herring port encircled by castles. A rugged coastal path leads out to St John's Point and a ruined tenth-century church. Watch out for an interesting eighteenth-century corbelled pigsty along the way.

To the west is Dundrum, another fishing village where Isambard Kingdom Brunel's SS *Great Britain*, an early steamship, ran aground taking a year to refloat. John de Courcy led the 1177 Norman invasion of east Ulster and built a motte and bailey castle here in 1210. Shortly afterwards King John come to visit to see the new fortification. Today the medieval ruins stand high on a natural defensive ridge revealing a circular keep and massive walls from which are stunning views over the water. Constructed over an earlier fortified earthwork or "dun," there are spiral staircases, parapets, drum towers and a gatehouse to explore. To relax after the steep hike to the castle above town, return to catch a game of skittles in a pub garden. This game is unique to the area and involves a circle of whittled, cut and painted broom handles.

Heading north is Ballynahinch. In 1798 the wide-streeted town was the scene of a decisive battle when 7,000 United Irishmen lost the rebellion cause. But the area is mostly visited to see the Legananny Dolmen nestled in the whale-back shaped drumlins on the slopes of Cratlieve Mountain to the south of town. A fine example of a Neolithic high-status burial, the long granite capstone is supported by two six-feet portal stones and a single support giving the dolmen a tripod appearance. Originally covered in earth, the stone skeleton of a tomb lies atmospherically in a brooding and desolate landscape. Silhouetted against a sunset or moody sky, the dolmen gives rise to much mystical and magical imaginings.

Nearby is Binder's Cove, an underground tomb or souterrain, at Finnis. This 30 metre-long passage grave is roughly a metre wide and half as much again high and so is very explorable with a torch. The dry stone walls follow through the central passage with two side chambers. Overhead is a roof of large, flat stone lintels. Walking into the heart of the earth in this room of the dead is a very atmospheric experience but best attempted during dry weather as it does flood during the rains.

STRUELL WELLS

Another atmospheric site with the imprint of the St Patrick legend is Struell Wells, a complex of five buildings, church and bathing houses, and a primary pilgrimage destination from the sixteenth century, if not before, through the nineteenth century. On Mid-Summer's Eve and the Friday before Lammas, hundreds of people flocked to the wells. And today the wells are still visited, less formally, by those seeking cures, although the modern flow of water is somewhat compromised. None of the original fourteenth century structures remain, current buildings date to the 1600s.

A fast moving stream flows through the rocky valley with the wells and the pilgrim buildings on its bank. There is the shell of an eighteenth-century church which appears to have never been finished. It replaced a thirteenth-century chapel. Some stone window fragments from this earlier building have been incorporated into the wall next to the Drinking Well, or Mother Well, a domed, bee-hive shaped vault. The central Eye Well, curing eye or sight problems, has a corbelled pyramid roof.

The Men's Bathing Well is a stone-roofed house with a seated dressing room and a bathing room with a sunken tank and sluice to control water flow. A less luxurious bathing well was for women. At a lower level, this shower-like room had water entering high up in the cubicle to drench the bathers before flowing out of a drain in the opposite wall. In the two primary wells the whole body was immersed but there are smaller wells for individual body parts such as head, arms and feet.

There is no historical evidence to support the tale but legend has it that St Patrick visited the wells to bathe and blessed the site singing psalms and holy songs. Past penitential rituals involved walking a complicated path on sharp stones circling the wells before rotating in a nearby stone Chair of St. Patrick followed by prayers and ending in the holy well bathing. This pilgrimage could be gruelling with some of the turn being on the knees over sharp pebbles and carrying a heavy stone. But in the nineteenth century reports of rowdy behaviour and raucous disturbance caused the authorities to ban organised devotional rituals and the popularity of the site waned. Visitors with spiritual and healing intent today come with quiet and private reverence and most people are just enjoying the historic shady hollow.

SKETRICK CASTLE

Loughside, mid-way up the western shore is Sketrick Castle. This large, four-storey tower house guarded the causeway to Sketrick Island and was actively involved in warfare in the sixteenth century. The immediacy and need for the defence is vitally evident in this watery landscape. The date of its construction is unknown but the Annals of the Four Masters record its capture in 1470.

Its square stateliness stayed intact until 1898 when a violent storm destroyed some of the structure taking out most of one wall so today's visitor can see a tower house sliced through. It had a boat bay and a lock-up. In medieval times the only way to get onto the island was to pass through a guarded narrow entrance passage at the base of the tower.

Excavations in the 1950s uncovered a subterranean passage to an underground spring with lintels running under the bawn courtyard wall to a corbel over the fresh drinking water.

View of Sketrick Castle across Strangford Lough.

NENDRUM MONASTIC SITE

Nearby, on another island now reached by a causeway of bridges linking submerged drumlins, is a site with a calmer heritage of tranquillity. The Nendrum monastic site is a romantic, hilltop reminder of early monastic life with stunning views across the lough. The hill is crowned with three concentric rings of dry-stone walled enclosures anchored by a church with a stone sundial and surrounded by monks' cells and graves, cross-slabs and with the stump of a round tower off to one side.

The origin of the monastery is unclear, but it is thought to have been founded by St Machaoi in the fifth century with the blessing of St. Patrick some years later. The ruins are now mostly very low stone walls, a visual floor plan of pre-Norman monastic life. The central enclosure is the heart of sacred life with huts and workshops in the middle enclosure and industrial work areas on the outside.

GIANT'S RING

Heading away from Strangford Lough towards Belfast and just before being engulfed by the bustle of the modern world is a prehistoric enclosure, awe inspiring due to its size. The Giant's Ring is 600 feet (200m) in diameter surrounded by a sturdy grass bank 15 feet (4.5m) high and averaging a width of around 20 feet (6m) which has a path on top to easily circumnavigate the site which has a dolmen at its centre. Bones have been excavated from this chambered burial tomb which has five uprights and a very large capstone.

The earthwork is a henge, a late Neolithic ceremonial site of assembly, and the largest known in Ireland. The outer embankment was created by scooping out the earth from the central arena. The surrounding area is littered with prehistoric monuments including cist burials and standing stones.

Recent excavation on the ridge to the north uncovered traces of a very large timber enclosure with buildings and burials. In Neolithic times this whole area was an exceptionally important sacred landscape and place of religio-political power. And the Giant's Ring was at its heart.

Over time the sturdy man-made creation has settled stalwartly into the scenery and was used as a horse racing track in the eighteenth century.

Sketrick Castle.

The dolmen at the heart of the Giant's Ring.

WHAT IS A MEGALITHIC STRUCTURE?

Across Northern Ireland there are many stone structures from the Neolithic Age which are called megalithic, *mega* means big and *lith* translates as stone. The stone circles are well known as being probable astronomical sites with alignment to sunrise or sunset at the summer or winter solstice honouring the rebirth of the sun and life.

But what of the well constructed Stone Age passage graves and stone tombs which we now see as pre-historic monuments with the framework of sturdy uprights and massive capstones standing mortarless and kept in place under their own weight some 5,000 years after their creation?

According to E.C. Krupp, astronomer and director of the Griffith Observatory in Los Angeles, they have an "astronomy-merged-with-funerary dimension." Excavation often finds interment of multiple people's ashes and bones. This is not a cemetery for everyone but for the selected elite few, noted not by burial with high status grave goods but the tomb being "a home for special spirits, it may be more accurate to understand it as a temple or shrine than as a grave."

Writing in *Skywatchers, Shamans and Kings*, Krupp likens the tombs to "birth chambers of the earth...like the womb of Mother Earth" with seasonal alignment to the sun.

But these are not astronomical observatories. They are a place of the dead and a "community shrine" needing the communal effort of a family or clan to erect these architecturally challenging structures.

The later Celts saw the abandoned stone structures as gateways to another world which gives rise to the fairyland stories such as at Ossian's Grave.

Giant's Ring.

CHAPTER 3

The Glens of the Antrim Coast

Entrance to the tower, Ballygalley Castle.

Heading north from the urban Belfast conurbation motorways give way to a rural road hugging the spectacular Antrim coast indented with stunning, silent glens terminating in unique fishing villages. One of the last places to have roads and the last area to speak Gaelic as the primary language, the Antrim coast is shrouded in the myths and legends from the pre-sixth century Dalriadic kings and passed down through the ages in the oral tradition of the shanachie story tellers.

The rugged coastline is sprinkled with mystery and imbued with history revealed in remains of raths, defensive cashels (small ring forts), crannogs and medieval churches. Stretching back from the seashore is a series of glens rich in folk lore of daring deeds, battles and love. This is the land of warrior poet Ossian, giant Finn McCool, Deirdre of the Sorrows and the Children of Lir who were turned into swans by a wicked stepmother being banished to fly for 300 years over the Sea of Moyle.

BALLYGALLEY AND GLENARM

The gateway to the nine glens, Ballygalley is home to one of the best-preserved seventeenth-century Scottish baronial plantation castles. Built in 1625 it is reputed to be one of the oldest inhabited buildings in Northern Ireland. Now a hotel with a resident ghost, visitors can fortify themselves in the cellars, the hotel's bar, before climbing the worn steps of the tower. At the top an appropriately creaky door opens onto a tiny, chilly turret room decorated with simple furnishings, the inhabitant having just left her bed. This is the Ghost Room. Reputedly, Lady Isobel Shaw, the wife of the original owner, jumped or was thrown from the window when she did not produce an heir. Ghost hunters have found two other spirits who wander the corridors at night and disembodied soldiers from yore sheltering from raids have been encountered in the garden.

Remains of external fortification in the garden of Ballygalley Castle.

Ghost room, Ballygalley Castle.

A wee step up the coast is the bright and cheery village of Glenarm, one of the oldest glen settlements, dating back to the thirteenth century. The narrow main street of Georgian houses and twisting side streets with colour-washed cottages have pavements with geometric patterns made from basalt and limestone cobbles.

Tucked to the rear of the village is Glenarm Castle, home of the Earl of Antrim. A private residence, the castle is not open to the public, although the walled eighteenth-century garden is, but the gateway leads into the much walked Glenarm Forest and provides a good view of this curious building which is like a mini Tower of London complete with pepper pot turrets. This eccentric Palladian mansion is an eighteenth century transformation of an earlier castle. The first castle and the family line were founded in the thirteenth century by a Scot who was escaping after killing someone in a tournament. He was meant to go to the Holy Land for penance but came to Glenarm instead.

Beach at Ballygalley.

Pavement of basalt and limestone, Glenarm.

Georgian architecture of Glenarm.

Above and below: *Layde Old Church.*

FROM CUSHENDALL TO CUSHENDUN

Know as the "capital of the glens," Cushendall celebrates traditional culture with an annual music and dance festival in mid-August. Behind the village is the fairy hill and stories of mischievous fairies abound. You will not catch anyone cutting down a fairy thorn, the hawthorn, in these parts for fear of bad luck.

Back up behind the village are the cliff-top ruins of Layde Old Church, the atmospheric fourteenth-century parish church, a place of worship from 1302 through to 1790. Reputed to have Franciscan foundations, the ruins show four phases of medieval reworkings. The long, narrow building once had a tower.

Quiet and meditative a fast-flowing steams brushes past Layde church creating a lush green arboreal resting place for the chiefs of the MacDonnell clan. Intriguing graveyard memorials are a reminder of the area's maritime roots and an ancient holed cross stands at the gate.

Looking on modern maps the parish is written as Layd but the local and commonly used spelling is the antiquarian spelling Layde.

Inland, high up on bleak moorland, megalithic monuments and raths dot the farms. The most dramatic is an oval stone court cairn, a multiple burial site from the Neolithic

farming aristocracy around 3,000BC. Romantically called Ossian's Grave, the site is named for the legendary warrior poet. Although, being an early Christian, Ossian lived many thousand years after the creation of this stone circle.

But fact never gets in the way of a good tale in this neck of the woods. And the mythology says that Ossian was the son of Finn, eater of the Salmon of Wisdom – but that is another story, and the goddess Sadb who had been changed into a deer. As a young man Ossian fell in love with the magical Niamh and they stole away to Tir Na Nog, the Land of the Ever Young, where he stayed for 300 years. And it is at this very site that, it is told, one can follow the golden-haired Niamh to the underworld fairyland.

Returning to the coast is the once fashionable resort and luxurious watering hole of Cushendun. Designed by Clough Williams-Ellis, creator of the fantasy Portmeirion in Wales, the village is most un-Irish having a Cornish feel. Built between 1912 and 1926 the village has white-washed stone cottages with slate roofs.

To the west of the village in Craigagh Wood is a rock carved with a crucifix that once served as an altar for clandestine masses in the eighteenth century. And nearby is the indented Gloonan Stone, the two depressions supposedly made by St Patrick's knees as he prayed. From the path to the woods catch glimpses of Cave House, a mansion set in a natural hilly amphitheatre and reached by a 60-feet-long tunnel through the red sandstone, and now a private Catholic retreat.

Cushendun.

NINE GLENS

'Up the airy mountain
Down the rushy glen,
We daren't go a-hunting
For fear of little men'
  - William Allingham

There are nine glens or hanging valleys. All are natural wonderlands of elemental beauty and worthy of exploration. During the summer the glen villages hold feis or fleadhs, festivals of traditional song and dance that were instigated at the start of the twentieth century during revitalisation of indigenous culture and folklore launched during Victorian times.

This area has a wild face and wilder reputation and was little settled by the plantation English. William Makepeace Thackeray, the nineteenth century novelist described the glens as "Switzerland in miniature."

Each individual glen is unique in character and the names reflect a description of the glen or events that happened in the glen. They are listed here from north to south.

Glentaisie is named after Taisie a princess from Rathlin Island, reputedly a great beauty with "bright cheeks," and sweeps down the western flank of Knocklayd mountain.

Glenshesk is called the sedgy glen or glen of reeds. Wooded, wild and unspoiled the glen is dotted with standing stones and monuments marking the passing of early saints and clan leaders.

Glendun is the wildest of the Antrim glens with a marvellous scenic walk through brown heather, which gives it the name of brown glen, and blazing yellow gorse. Deep sided with steep inclines and deciduous woodland, an "Altar in the Wood" is hidden amongst the trees. This rock is carved with scenes from the crucifixion and dates from the seventeenth century when Catholics attended mass in secret to avoid the Penal Laws. A stately, red brick 1836 viaduct spans the glen.

Glencorp is a gently sloped and small glen named for the slaughter of a forgotten battle. There are signs of early habitation including a Bronze Age barrow burial mound known as The Fort and defended Christian rath farmsteads.

Glenaan is a steep sided gorge with the stone circle grave of Osin (Ossian) at its head. Called "glen of the fords," it was once a vibrant rural community with farming, spinning and weaving, a shoemaker as well as corn, tuck and flax mills. A deserted village with the roofless wallsteads of former houses attest to a population now gone, replaced by sheep and cattle and the occasional peat cutter.

Glenballyeamon, the town of Eamon or Edwardstown is a wide but deep glen. Enclosures of worked ditches and banks are the remnants of former occupation and there is an old Stone Age flint factory where many axe heads have been uncovered.

Glenariff is known as the ploughman's glen and is the most spectacular with the Mare's Tail waterfall. Dramatic precipices with mature native woodland of oak, ash and hazel make this a very attractive place which is often called "Queen of the Glens." It is reached from Glenariff Forest Park with a five mile walk along the Waterfall Trail.

Glencoy is the glen of hedges or dykes and, because of its shape, it is also called "Glen of the Sword." It descends to the pretty harbour of Carnlough Bay with a distinctive white chalk arch. This is the land of the O'Donnells, where the Marchioness of Londonderry built the Londonderry Arms Hotel, an ivy covered old coaching station. A bedroom is named in honour of Sir Winston Churchill, a previous owner who inherited the property.

Glenarm is known as the glen of the army and is reached by a forested trail from the charming Glenarm village. Excavations have unearthed Stone Age tombs as well as Iron Age raths and souterrain passage graves. It is reputed that Shane O'Neill is buried here minus his head which was left on a spike outside Dublin Castle.

Glenarm Castle.

DISTANCE: 6 miles (9.5 kilometres).

ALLOW: 3 hours.

DIFFICULTY: Leisurely with incline up out of Cushendall and easily walked paths and back roads.

FACILITIES: Refreshments and toilets in all three villages

TRANSPORT: Buses run along the coastal road.

Start at Waterfoot village at the mouth of the Glenariff glen and proceed north with the crashing ocean waves to your right. Continue past the shops and cottages lining the single main road.

The path is marked with an Ulster Way sign travelling to the west of Waterfoot with views across the harbour and past the ruins of Red Arch Castle perched above Red Bay.

At Cushendall follow the main road as it winds through the pretty village and passes by the early nineteenth century look-out Curfew Tower built to confine riotous prisoners. Continue over the river then branch off to the right and right again at the fork beyond the village taking the cliff walk until meeting the road at Layde Church. The romantic ruin is worth a detour.

Continue along this quiet road of farms and woodland until turning right onto the B92 for the last lap into the elegant white-washed village of Cushendun.

Layde Old Church.

CHAPTER 4

The Dramatic North Coast

The north coast is a holidaymaker's honey pot with beach resorts, dramatic coastal scenery, romantic castles and intriguing ruins.

First up when turning west from the glens is the serene Bonamargy Friary nestled as a small, wild oasis in the spreading greens of Ballycastle golf course.

This Third Order of Franciscan Friary was founded in 1485 by the MacQuillan family. Julie MacQuillen known as "The Black Nun" resided here. She was a renowned seventeenth-century prophet, ascetic and recluse and reputedly asked to be buried at the entrance of the chapel so she might be underfoot of all who entered there. Her grave is marked by a cross with a round hole. The MacDonnell aristocracy who valiantly challenged the invading forces of Queen Elizabeth I, including Sorely Boy MacDonnell, are also buried here. Coffins line the vault, the English, Latin and Irish inscriptions outlining the changing cultural waves of Irish history. In the surrounding cemetery there are many interesting gravestones including an old skull and crossbones carved on a lichen-laden slab and memorials to sailors who died at sea.

Approached through a gatehouse set in an earth bank, the church is now roofless and missing an end wall but the long narrow structure is solid still. Damaged in warfare in the sixteenth century it was repaired and used through the seventeenth century. It takes little imagination to visualise the extent of the building and the religious community living here. There are visual hints of what would have stood such as the lean-to corbels for wooden cloisters still visible in the stone walls.

And although historic it is still a holy site. A prayer cloth rag tied to the remnant of the round hole cross shows the power and contemporary vitality of the place.

Bonmargy Friary.

Bonmargy Friary.

Black Nun Cross at Bonmargy Friary.

Skull and crossbone grave at Bonmargy Friary.

Gateway to Bonamargy Friary.

Ballycastle.

BALLYCASTLE AND RATHLIN ISLAND

Ballycastle is an attractive resort town, developed in the 1700s its eighteenth century origins are evident in the architecture of the houses, many of which are now guesthouses, and classic parish church. The town comes alive with the Auld Lammas Fair held every year on the last Monday and Tuesday of August. This is the only remaining of six fairs granted by charter in 1606 and has a traditional flavour with sheep and pony sales and edible seaweed treats. Well experienced in festivities, the town also hosts a three-day Gaelic Games every June after the Northern Lights Festival of music and dance in May.

Ballycastle's claim to more recent historic fame is that in 1898 technology pioneer Guglielmo Marconi tested wireless from here with the first commercial transmission to Rathlin Island some 8 miles (13km) offshore. A plaque in the marina marks the spot. And a daily 45-minute boat trip to Rathlin leaves the town in the morning returning in the afternoon.

Marconi Memorial.

Stepping ashore this small, wild and isolated L-shaped island some eight by two miles, called Raghery by locals, one steps back into a carless past. Rathlin is still farmed with old agricultural methods amongst small grazing and hay fields, traditional farmhouses, kelp processing and bogs illuminated by a haze of darting dragonflies.

The island is best known for the cave where Robert Bruce holed up in 1306. And it was here he watched the spider and penned that homily on perseverance: "if you don't first succeed, try, try and try again." And empowered by patience, he was inspired to return to Scotland to fight and win the famous battle at Bannockburn regaining his crown. But a boat is needed to visit the cave.

On foot one can see the stone sweat house at Knockams, a prehistoric mound fort known as Doonmore near the Stone Age settlement at Brookley and a Celtic standing stone east of the harbour. Then, after being buffeted by fierce, salty winds on this treeless rock, retreat to the pub.

View over to Rathlin Island.

There are many tales to hear from the warmth of the snug bar about this island that was the first Irish landfall for the raiding Vikings in 795. In 1575 the English came ashore and slaughtered the women and children of the MacDonnell clan who had been secreted on Rathlin for their safety. And in 1642 it was here the Scottish Campbells butchered the men.

Rathlin was a major exporter of flint axes during the Mesolithic era and the island was fought over, won and lost and won again, by the Vikings and Normans as well as the Scots and English. Scotland and Ireland battled for ownership of Rathlin and it was decided in favour of Ireland because it had no snakes – a decision based on St Patrick supposedly banishing all snakes from Ireland in the fifth century.

There are fine views of Rathlin Island and over to the Scottish Isles from Fair Head where wild goats roam. A pace back from the cliff is Lough na Cranagh with a crannog, a manmade island, dating from the early Christian period.

CARRICK-A-REDE BRIDGE

A perilous, windswept rope bridge hangs some 80 feet (30m) above a churning cauldron of a sea. Local fishermen have kept a seasonal bridge, a spider's web of rope and planks, over to Carrick Island since the 1600s. The last local fishermen retired in 2002 and the 60 feet (20m) span over to the offshore rock, which is a nesting ground for seabirds, is maintained by the National Trust. The original single hand rail bridge with wide slats has been replaced by a much safer dual hand rail, caged bridge.

Carrick-a-Rede means "rock in the road," the road being the salmon pathway past the coast to their spawning ground. Every spring the fishermen strung the bridge across this coastal chasm to catch the migrating Atlantic salmon, the sea being too rough to reach by boat. They emptied the bag nets every day through the autumn when the bridge would be taken down.

The walk over is not for those with vertigo. But as the structure gently twists with the rhythm of footfall best not to look down. Instead, look up at the kittiwakes, cormorants and guillemots noisily wheeling overhead. To truly savour the wildness of the experience go early in the morning or out of season as there are long queues and crowds in the summer.

Boat trips from nearby Ballintoy give a great view of the bridge and under cliff caves from the sea travelling by way of Sheep Island, a steep-sided and flat-topped sea stack

Carrick-a-Rede Bridge.

which is a hideaway for puffins. The small fishing harbour is a brisk step from the village down a very small, very narrow, very steep road plunging down Knocksaughey Hill past the entrance to the Carrick-a-Rede Bridge and the Carrick-a-Rede Hotel. Stone quays are built to enhance the natural rock formations that reach out into the sea like arms embracing this modest and attractive harbour overlooked by the distinctive white church on the brow of the hill above. The quiet, isolated atmosphere is a calming antidote to the bustle of the Carrick-a-Rede Bridge.

DUNSEVERICK CASTLE

On a narrow peninsular stretching onto the sea from the cliffs of Benbane stand the crumbling crenalations of a romantic castle keep. Although only the gatehouse now defiantly remains, Dunseverick Castle is an atmospheric reminder of the harshness of life in the Middle Ages when the Irish chiefs had to battle defending land and clan.

Dunseverick Castle.

From 500 to 800 this was the capital of the kingdom of Dalriada and the terminus of one of the five great royal roads radiating out from Tara, the ancient seat of the kings of Ireland. The original stone fort was attacked by the Viking raiders in 870 and it was from here that the fifth-century Irish raids were launched on Scotland. St Patrick was reputedly a regular visitor to the castle.

So strong was it as a defensive position that General Robert Munro and his Cromwellian troops found it necessary to raze it to the ground during the seventeenth-century Irish rebellion. But the walls were too thick, although the damage made it untenable as a residence and it was vacated in 1657. And it is to the eroding ravages of the sea that the castle now surrenders as the ocean chips away at the cliff foundations. Its charm is only increased by its precariousness.

A short walk along the beach below is Portbradden, a hamlet perilously wedged in a rocky cleft between towering cliff and thrashing sea with four houses and a little church, reputedly the smallest in Ireland. There are fossils on the beach, occasionally salmon fishing nets still float out from the shore and there are the remains of a Stone Age settlement at the edge of the bay.

BUSHMILLS, DUNLUCE CASTLE, PORTRUSH AND ON TO MUSSENDEN TEMPLE

As Bushmills has been distilling whiskey since 1608, a trip to visit its tasting rooms can have historic validity. Whiskey means "water of life" and, in the name of historic research, sip single malt, aged for decades in casks seasoned with sherry, bourbon and Madeira and be revitalised.

Bushmills Distillery.

Apart from the spelling, the difference between Scottish whisky and Irish whiskey is scotch is only distilled twice whereas Irish whiskey is distilled three times. Spirits have been brewed on this spot for centuries before the seventeenth century when the distilling license was granted. And the longevity of the successful production is captured in the Bushmills' strap line: "It's not because the distillery is old that the whiskey is good... It's because the whiskey is good that the distillery is old."

Along the coast to the west is Dunluce Castle which clings to a crag surrounded by the sea, reached by a bridge across a 20-foot chasm above jagged rocks. Below and underneath the castle is a huge cave which can be visited by boat. Once a stronghold of the MacDonnells, Lords of the Isles, only two thirteenth-century towers and the ruins of a great hall built in the 1500s remain. In 1584 Dunluce was battered by the English troops. The Irish reclaimed the castle, the defending forces being pulled 100 feet up from the sea in baskets.

In 1588 a storm swept the Spanish Armada galleon *Girona* onto the rocks with rich pickings coming from the wreck. Thirteen hundred people drowned that night including members of Spain's most notable and noble families. A few years later the castle's kitchen crumbled into the sea during another storm taking the cooks along with it and the family abandoned the hilltop fortification. And it has stood since then slowly crumbling into a romantic ruin that inspired Thackeray to write:

> *Standing upon a leaden rock and looking as if some old, old princess of old, old fairy times were dragon-guarded within.*

Nearby Portrush is a rowdy, fun fair kind of a seaside town and good for family fun on the two sandy beaches. Along the rock strewn coast is Portstewart, a more genteel Victorian resort, with a two-mile Strand and an excellent surf break.

On the western edge of the north coast, perched on a cliff edge above Magilligan Strand is the Mussenden Temple. This eccentric, domed summer library was constructed by an unorthodox bishop as a memorial to his wife in 1783. Although an Anglican he invited Catholic mass to be said in his architectural folly. Modelled on the Roman Temple of Vesta, Mussenden is a fantasy built of basalt and faced in limestone with three windows and a door pointing to each of the four compass points.

Nearby, on the mouth of the River Bann is the earliest known inhabited place in Ireland. There is not much to see of the settlement of hunter gatherer fishermen from 7000BC but a mound and a few post holes.

DISTANCE: 5 miles (8 kilometres).

ALLOW: 2–3 hours walking plus hours looking.

DIFFICULTY: Moderate with many climbs and descents. Can be windy and blustery, walk with protective dress and stout shoes.

FACILITIES: Refreshments and toilets at Giant's Causeway.

TRANSPORT: Buses run along the coastal road, irregular.

Start at the crumbling ruins of medieval Dunseverick Castle, the old home base of the MacDonnell clan. Legend has it that resident Conal Caernach witnessed the crucifixion of Christ while serving with the Roman army. Take the staircase down to the coastal path lined with colourful wildflowers visited by flutters of butterflies and interesting insects. Proceed along the dramatic cliffs with screeching gulls overhead and waves crashing along the rocks to Portmoon.

Between Bengore Head and Benbane is Hamilton's Seat and at 100 metres above sea level it is the highest point of the Causeway cliff path with stunning sea views. Formidable tides run offshore and great seas can swiftly and dramatically build up. Follow the headlands with waves crashing onto rocky bays below, enjoy views over Port-na-Spaniagh where galleon *Girona* foundered in 1588 (the salvaged golden treasure trove is on display at the Ulster Museum in Belfast). Carry on past rock formations aptly named with descriptive titles such as Chimney Tops, Giant's Eye and a range of 40 feet high basalt columns called Organ Pipes. The combination of white chalk, roaring sea, moorland pathways and beach, all crafted by Ice Age erosion, laced with a bracing sea breeze make this an

Dunseverick Castle – start of walk.

invigorating ramble. Keep your eyes open for some rare plant species including a type of orchid called "Irish lady's tresses."

Nearing the end of the walk a deep stone Shepherd's Stairway descends to the stunning natural spectacle of the Giant's Causeway to the left. Pass the "giant's boot" a large boot-shaped rock on the foreshore. Then continue through the Giant's Gate to enjoy the Stepping Stone, the Wishing Chair close to the water's edge and the dramatic field of some 37,000 pillars of mostly hexagonal, (some have as many as ten sides) black basalt columns striding out into the sea from a sandy shore, plunging under the waves to reappear in Scotland.

Known as the Eighth Wonder of the World, declared one of the natural wonders of the world by the Royal Geographical Society and one of the only UNESCO World Heritage Sites in Ireland, the Giant's Causeway was created sixty million years ago as the flowing lava from a volcanic eruption cracked into these amazing shapes. But local tour guides know better and the stone formations have names given by the Victorians because this geological mystery was really created as stepping stones by the giant Finn McCool. There are many amusing tall tales with one rock being his grandmother, another his camel.

Then it is a slow but gradual climb up to the visitor centre, past

Giant's Causeway at the end of the walk.

the old 1920s school which is now a museum and onto the main road and a bus route. But first take refreshment at the Causeway Hotel and follow in the footsteps of Victorian writer William Makepeace Thackeray who visited the site in 1842. At first he was not impressed with the scene but after a tot of whiskey declared "when the world was moulded and fashioned out of formless chaos, this must have been the bit left over – a remnant of chaos."

This walk is only a small segment of the waymarked Causeway Coast Way, a track which runs for 32 miles (52km) along the north coast between Portstewart and Ballycastle and so your hike can be extended in either direction. The entire, mostly cliff top, path has stunning views of bays and beaches with a chain of castles along the way and interesting plants, birds and marine life. And stories from the legend of Finn MacCool, the tale of Spanish Armada shipwreck, the ancient history of the Kingdom of Dalriada and the mysteries of the Bronze Age stone monuments keep the hiker inspired.

Causeway Museum at the end of the walk.

The Causeway Coast.

Causeway Hotel at the end of the walk.

CHAPTER 5

Derry and the Plantation Heartland

DERRY

In 546 people fled from the plague in Donegal to take refuge on the banks of the Foyle. In their midst was a monk, St Columba, who founded a monastery here that rose to importance in the twelfth century before being burnt by the Vikings in 1195. The name of the place was Doire, which means an oak grove surrounded by peat bog. The name evolved to Derry. And later became Londonderry.

Destroyed in 1608 by Cahir O'Doherty, it was rebuilt by James I to become the bastion of Protestant rule as English Protestant colonists were granted huge tracts of land by the king called plantations. The English added the name London to the city and it became Londonderry, the jewel in the crown of the Plantation Society. And the name, is it Derry or Londonderry, is in contention to this day.

The second largest city of Northern Ireland and one of the longest inhabited places in Ireland, it is known as the Maiden City of Derry because its walls have never been breached. The walls, which are 25 feet high and 28 feet thick, withstood the 1641 rebellion and the Cromwellian wars of 1649. But it is the 105 day siege in 1689 which is the most famous.

The longest siege in British history started as the Catholic Jacobite forces of James II, the last Stuart king who was attempting to re-capture the English throne, blockaded the Protestant troops of the newly installed monarch, William of Orange. For fifteen weeks the inhabitants were trapped, barricaded in the city. And a quarter of the 30,000 inhabitants died, the survivors living on a menu of dogs, horse and rats reputedly "fattened on the flesh of dead Irish." The image of a skeleton is on the city's coat of arms in tribute to the siege.

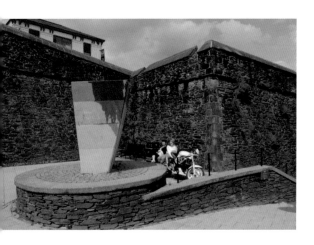

Derry's Walls.

The stalwart walls and defensive ramparts are constructed of local limestone and building materials from ruined monasteries and can be walked today. The entire city can be encircled on foot with views from the top of the walls down over the city with its, largely still intact, Renaissance street plan. The route passes watchtowers, the original four gates with defensive drawbridges and portcullis as well as the three other gates added at later dates. On 12 August there is the annual parade around the walls in honour of the thirteen Apprentice Boys who saved the day and closed Ferryquay Gate against the Jacobite army.

Much blighted by The Troubles, today Derry is restored with building and restoration work going on throughout the city and returning to the cultural strength that inspired

Derry's walls – Ferryquay Gate was closed by the Apprentice Boys against the Jacobites during the siege of 1689.

nineteenth-century historian Thomas Carlyle to describe it as "the prettiest looking town." Visitors can explore the city's history in the award-winning Tower Museum near Guildhall Square. The Harbour Museum is worth a trip to see the thirty-feet long replica of the curragh sailed by St Columba and the Derry Craft Village in Shiphay Street is a recreation of a traditional stone village with craft shops.

MAGHERA AND THE PLANTATION HEARTLAND

When King James I organised the colonisation of Northern Ireland he established The Honourable The Irish Society in 1613 to oversee the plantation system dividing these rich farmlands among the English. The society is still going strong although now stripped of any political clout it is still responsible for maintaining the Derry walls.

The imprint of the plantation system maps the agricultural Derry hinterland along with traces of older societies. After the bustle of Derry and the well-trod tourist coastal paths, the rural interior is a peaceful patchwork of fertile fields and farming country with undulating rolling hills laced with hiking and nature trails.

Sheep – the rural plantation heartland.

Maghera is a charming town at the heart of the plantation lands with an old church on the site of a sixth century monastery. The tower dates from the 1600s but the twelfth-century west door is a picture book of animal and floral designs.

But the magic of Maghera is a short distance from town. Tirnony Dolmen is an enchanting site. The dolmen sits solidly and happily in the field and wooded landscape with a free standing orthostat stone derivative of the court tomb tradition. The capstone sits at a jaunty angle above the well-defined square chamber.

The region is spattered with attractive plantation towns including Magherafelt with Springhill, a whitewashed, tall-roofed seventeenth-century manor house now owned by the National Trust. Lived in for generations of the Lenox-Conyngham family from its construction in 1680, the laundry houses an extensive costume collection. Its more famous resident is the ghost of the Blue Room. This female phantom is reputed to retrace her rush to, unsuccessfully, stop the gunshot of her suicidal husband shamed by an army court marshal in 1814.

Tirnony Dolmen, Maghera.

Bellaghy is a circular defensive town with a castle and bawn courtyard dating back to 1622. Nobel Prize winning poet Seamus Heaney narrates the local museum exhibition. And there are magical walks in the sixty-acre wooded estate at Ballyscullion Park, a Georgian House and stables on the banks of Lough Beg.

Draperstown was created by the London Company of Drapers in 1618. As its name implies there was an interest here in cloth. And the cloth was linen. Irish linen is world renowned for being the very finest material. The industry originated with cottagers working in their homes as a family concern. The business expanded developing into highly organised production in large mills with workers, mostly women, spinning and weaving for very long hours, in very harsh conditions, with very little remuneration. Today one can step into the thundering cacophony of the linen industry at Wellbrook Beetling Mill. Dating from 1765, this water-powered mill was used in the final manufacture of linen, a polishing procedure called beetling. Costumed guides lead tours through the scotching, hackling and weaving processes, the noise a contrast to the quiet woodland outside.

A good map is essential while travelling in Northern Ireland but the page comes alive when talking to local people who become essential, willing and helpful guides when seeking out sites. But things are never easy. The Draperstown of the map becomes Ballinascreen when on the ground. Whatever its name, the small town is the gateway to the blue-tinged, heather-clad Sperrin Mountains.

An area rich in archaeological interest from standing stones, stone circles and chambered graves to raths and a pre-historic sweat house, the North Sperrin Heritage Trail has Dungiven at its hub. On a bluff overlooking the river at the edge of town are the remains of a twelfth-century Augustinian Priory housing the finest medieval tomb with ornate tracery and kilted warriors. Although a ruin, the site is vitally alive with modern veneration. Along the path to the Priory there is a holy well in a smooth boulder. This is a "wart-well." A strip of cloth is dipped in the water, wiped on a wart then tied to a tree to banish the growth. The same procedure also reputedly gives relief to arthritis and rheumatism sufferers. And there stands today a stunted tree festooned with a flutter of rag flags, votive prayers for health, made from socks, handkerchiefs and assorted colourful scraps of cloth.

Braving the barking, but fortunately tethered, border collie in the farmyard it is a short scramble to Banagher Old Church, on a picturesque, twisting lane driving south of Dungiven. These impressive, sturdy ruins are of a church founded around 1100 by a local saint named Muiredach O'Heney who was led to the site by a stag. The saint is

Opposite: *Sperrin Mountains.*

Saint's mortuary, Banagher Old Church.

buried in a well-preserved mortuary in the churchyard. The tomb house stands on a sandy hill and superstition recommends grabbing a handful of sand to bring yourself and loved ones good luck.

The church was a ruin by 1622 but the strong, square-headed doorway with massive lintels has kept the structure sound. The historical records note a bloody event in 1121 when the King of Ciannacht was murdered in the cemetery by a kinsman. At the entrance to the site is a water-filled bullaun stone with a deep, spherical depression like a mortar waiting for a pestle.

Bullaun stones are often found at old ecclesiastical sites and it is assumed they have a religious significance, but their function is not clear nor fully understood. Some speculate that they were part of Bronze Age rituals and were adopted into Christian worship by the early church. They were reputedly used as mass rocks during the Penal Times, 1691 through to 1760. It is possible that they were purely functional and used for grinding food or dyes. More sinister suggestions equate them with human sacrifice from a pre-Christian era. The rainwater that collects in the hollow is said to have curative powers similar to holy wells.

Window, Banagher Old Church.

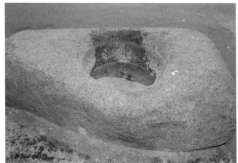

Bullaun stone.

THE NORTH SPERRINS HERITAGE TRAIL

This driving Heritage Trail traces fourteen sites embracing history, culture and, superstition with medieval castles, early Christian places of worship and megalithic stone monuments. The official Trail Guide can be picked up from local Tourist Information Centres. The creation of this trail and presentation of the sites is a generous collaboration between the Feeny Community Association, from the pleasant local village of Feeny, and local landowners as most of these sites are on private lands. However, dogs, even on leads, are not welcome as many of the sites are on working agricultural land with grazing sheep and cattle.

With an early start all the sites can be visited in one pretty busy and frenetic day. Or select the sites of particular interest then move on. Or be tempted to linger for a few days and meander with leisure. All sites have parking within walking distance.

Sperrin Mountains.

Starting at Drumcovitt House near the village of Feeny. This eighteenth-century, four-storey farmhouse was built by the Fishmongers' Company of London. The youngest of the ancient sites on the trail, it is now a private house. It can be viewed from the lay-by or stay here in the barns converted to self-catering accommodation.

Head southwest to Tandragee Fort, a rath or ringed fort reached through a field. The enclosing earthen bank sprouts hawthorn blackthorn and gorse making a "fairy ring." Being on high ground there are fabulous views across the glen onto the Sperrin Mountains and it overlooks the ruins of an old flax mill from the linen industry.

Carry on down the road to Ballydonegan Sweathouse, reached through a farmyard. Very popular in the eighteenth century it was like a sauna, steam room or Turkish Bath and was a cure for fevers and relief of muscle pain.

Banagher Old Church.

Backtrack and take the B40, turning swiftly left and park in tight against the hedgerow to enjoy the Aughlish Stone Circle from the late Neolithic–early Bronze Age. This is the primary area for the mysterious stone circles in Northern Ireland. A dramatic site, Aughlish has five stone circles and five alignment stones in what is commonly considered to be an astronomical arena.

Continue along country lanes to Banagher Old Church, a late eleventh early-twelfth century ecclesiastical site with dedicated car park. An impressive ruin the grounds house the mortuary tomb of St Muireach O'Heaney.

Retrack over the T-junction to the Megalithic Carnanbane Court Tomb, the remains of a two-chambered grave, access from lay-by.

It is a straight run to Dungiven Castle. Constructed in 1839 on the site of any early fortified house it can be viewed from the car park. Turn right out of town on the A6 to the medieval ecclesiastic site of Dungiven Priory. On a scenic site above the River Roe, the chancel contains the ornate fifteenth tomb of a local chieftan who died in 1385 and considered to be an outstanding example of its kind.

Go back into town and carry on straight to Bovevagh Old Church and graveyard dating back to medieval times with a tomb credited to St Ringan. Park tight on the road.

It is a winding journey east to the much-ruined Tannyranny Church a Roman Catholic church from the Penal Period. Park at Galvin school on the B64 and approach along 1km track.

Continue northwest on the B64 to the ceremonial Gortnamoyagh Inaugeration Stone reached by a short walk through the Gortnamoyagh Forest. Two elbow holes and two footprints make a cruciform shape in this basalt outcrop. It is linked to the Gaelic chieftains and was thought to be in use during inauguration ceremonies through the sixteenth century but there are many tales and legends connected to its use and origin.

At the next turn at Ballintemple is the early Christian Errigal Glen Church and Souterrain. Believed to have been founded by St Adamnan, the site is now a ruined medieval church in a walled graveyard. Adjacent to the church is a multi-chambered souterrain. Parking in lay-by.

The last stop is a rath called Kings Fort to the west on a winding country road. Nestled comfortably below the summit of Donald's Hill this substantial defensive site has revealed little about its past but would have been inhabited by high status warriors and clan elders.

This is the end of the ordered tour but for the adventurous who want to keep going there are other, less well marked sites to the east including Knockoneill Court Tomb, Carntogher Cairn and Slaughtneil Giant's Grave.

CHAPTER 6

The Ulster American Experience

In the 1700s the first flood of emigrants to the United States was not impoverished Catholic farmers but well funded, enterprising Presbyterian Protestants. Largely drawn from Derry and Omagh, the next wave of emigration to America and Canada in the eighteenth and nineteenth centuries was not so much the starving, driven off the land by famine, but younger sons of wealthy families who were looking to make a fortune and travelling with a substantial nest egg under their belts.

Imbued with an ethic of hard work, an independent spirit, and a distrust of government these early settlers created a founding plank of the American national character. Raised in the Protestant ethos of William of Orange, these acolytes of King William, known as King Billy, pushed westwards through the American continent to become the Hill Billies spawning the likes of Davy Crockett, Kit Carson and Jim Bowie. Eleven US presidents and half the signatories of the American Declaration of Independence had an Ulster pedigree.

THE ULSTER AMERICAN FOLK PARK

For many of the emigrants the streets were paved with gold. And some of the Ulstermen and their descendants found the riches and wealth that they had hoped to find in the New World including the likes of the Gettys and the Mellons. And the Mellon family and Mellon Foundation are so happy to honour the influence of their Ulster roots (ancestor Thomas Mellon emigrated from this area in 1818) that they created the Ulster American Folk Park near Omagh.

This exceptional open air living history museum is an amalgam of some thirty buildings both original structures relocated to the park – including the tiny, dark one-roomed

Bred with a strong Scots-Presbyterian work ethic many Ulstermen sought to make their fortune in North America. And Northern Ireland lays claim to eleven US presidents with direct ancestral lineage to the region: Andrew Jackson, James Knox Polk, James Buchanan, Andrew Johnson, Ulysees S. Grant, Chester Alan Arthur, Grover Cleveland, Benjamin Harrison, William McKinley, Theodore Roosevelt and Woodrow Wilson.

You must be born in the USA to become president and, amazingly, three of these, Jackson, Buchanan and Arthur, were first generation Americans. That is, their father was born in Ulster. Jackson only just making the qualification to be President being born shortly after his parents landed.

In all, one third of American presidents can trace roots to Ulster. Those with only some Ulstermen blood in their veins: Richard Milhous Nixon, John Quincy Adams, John Adams, Dwight D. Eisenhower, Harry S. Truman, Jimmy Carter, Bill Clinton and both Bushes.

The region produced both the creator and the printer as well as many of the signers of the American Declaration of Independence.

Eighteenth century single room cabin – moved from Altahoney, Sperrin Mountains.

Replica of Mellon's Church.

TO THE GLORY OF GOD
AND IN MEMORY OF
PAUL MELLON, K.B.E.
1907 - 1999

Mellon Memorial in Mellon's Church.

eighteenth century cottage moved from the nearby Sperrin Mountains and a schoolhouse – and replica buildings such as the thatched, whitewashed Mellon family Presbyterian meeting house which has a memorial stone to Paul Mellon, 1907–1999.

Anchoring the atmospheric wooded site is the actual restored birthplace and boyhood home of Judge Thomas Mellon, founder of the Pittsburgh banking dynasty. Ducks and chickens waddle past and nest in the well-stocked farmyard and an aromatic peat fire blazes in the hearth of the generously appointed, whitewashed and thatched stone cottage which stands unaltered in its original place.

The Park reconstructs the lives of the magnate Mellon family's origins in Ulster and also in the New World with their log homestead from Pennsylvania. Both are testaments to thrift and hard work.

A realistic portrayal of the transition of the eighteenth century Irish emigrant to America originating in the Ulster village, the arboreal pathways of the Park are bisected by the urban reconstruction of the docks on both sides of the Atlantic with a printer running sailing schedules from a heavy press in Ireland and a replica of the original Mellon Bank on the Pennsylvania side.

In between the Old and the New worlds there is the Atlantic transitional link of a cramped shipboard experience before stepping out into life in a Pennsylvanian village. Here are a range of New World house types, including an original log cabin farmstead with corn crib, smoke house and an active patchwork sewing bee going on inside and also the austere stone home of Samuel Fulton, a 1724 emigrant, that have both been shifted from Pennsylvania to Omagh.

Throughout, well costumed guides in period costumes demonstrate crafts and skills from candle making to fish salting and cooking with foodstuffs appropriate to the regions. The bellowed heat and harsh hammering of the forge draw the attention and it is hard to get past some lessons at the schoolhouse on the Old World side whereas the allure of the blueberry muffin baking aromas on the New are hard to pass up.

The Centre celebrates all the North American festivals and is a riot of activity on Independence Day, July 4th. And there is a massive hootenanny at the back end of summer with the Annual Bluegrass Festival.

Adjacent to the Park is the academic Centre for Migration Studies. Researching genealogists pore over documents alongside visiting American family history fans. The

Mellon House in original situation.

Blair's Printers, moved from Strabane.

Patchwork – US side.

Fulton House, shipped from Pennsylvania.

Forge – Ulster side.

Schoolhouse, Castletown – moved here, on the Ulster side.

Baking muffins – on the US side.

Playing horseshoes on the US side.

Crockery, Ulster side.

Ulster parlour.

library houses an Irish Emigration Database, emigrants' letters, passenger lists and newspaper articles. There is an ongoing culling of information from both sides of the Atlantic constantly swelling the pool of knowledge.

THE USA AND ULSTER CONNECTION TRAIL

Northern Ireland is lassoed with locations that have American connections from names on a map with a Presidential association to well tended heritage centres. This is a list of places with a US interest; the pilgrimage more or less runs clockwise from the Park.

STRABANE

John Dunlap printed America's first newspaper, *The Pennsylvania Packet*, and also was the printer of the American Declaration of Independence. He was born in Meeting House Street, Strabane, in 1746. He learned his trade as an apprentice at Gray's Printers whose

Peat burning fireplace of Ulster.

Below: *Campbell House, built 1786 and moved here, Ulster side.*

Right: *Wool preparation, Ulster side.*

Below: *Wagon, US side.*

Georgian façade still survives on Strabane's main street. The ink galleys and wheeling whirls of the presses, one with the heraldic American bald eagle, of the old printing works have been preserved by the National Trust.

DERGALT

James Wilson, grandfather of Woodrow Wilson, the 28th President of the United States of America, lived in Dergalt near Strabane. James Wilson was a printer by trade and in 1807, aged 20, he emigrated to Philadelphia becoming a prominent journalist and founding the *Pennsylvania Advocate*. By 1816 he was active in politics serving in the Ohio Legislature.

His home, The Wilson House, is open to the public and maintained by the Ulster American Folk Park in its original setting. The thatched, white-washed Woodend Cottage was one of a cluster of small, traditional farmhouses on the slopes of the Sperrin Mountains and is a humble dwelling. Descendants of the Wilson family farmed this land until recent times and there is much original furniture, kitchen utensils and farm implements still in place. The parlour doubles as a bedroom with a curtain for privacy, although the sleeping nook in the back of the kitchen by the hearth looks toastier.

COWANCOR

Nearby is Cowancor, the ancestral home of 11th president James Knox Polk. There is no residue of him or his family but that which imagination can provide.

CASTLEBERG CASTLE

Castleberg Castle has a very short history being built in 1619 and destroyed a couple of decades later in the rebellion of 1641. But today it houses an exhibition to native sons frontiersman and adventurer Davy Crockett, including his last stand in the Alamo in 1836, and President Adams whose ancestors came from this area.

DERRY

The emigration exodus fuelled the growth of the port of Londonderry as tens of thousands of people left for America in the eighteenth century also heading out to

England, Canada and Australia. The Harbour Museum preserves the prow of *Minnehaha*, the last sailing ship to run scheduled services to America. Even during the Civil War she delivered thousands of emigrants safely to New York.

DREEN

The aroma of soda bread baked over an open peat fire on a cobbled hearth by ladies in period costume wafts from the thatched cottage at Dreen, near Cullybrackley, welcoming visitors to the ancestral home of 21st US President Chester Arthur, 1881–5. His father left this house with its clay floor and open flax-straw roof to set sail for America in 1815. And his son inherited his talent as a salmon fisherman.

CONAGHER

The 25th President, William McKinley, had ancestral ties to Conagher near Ballymoney but there is little to note the heritage.

CARRICKFERGUS

In 1765 the Jacksons left Bonneybefore, Carrickfergus arriving in the Carolinas just in time for Andrew Jackson to be born on American soil enabling him to become the 7th US President, 1829–37. Their original home was destroyed in 1880 to make way for the railway; a blue plaque on a stone plinth marks the spot where the modest cottage once stood.

Nearby, the Andrew Jackson Centre is in a similar eighteenth century thatched farm cottage and honours the fiery hero of the Battle of New Orleans who was known as the "People's President." Furnished in the style of the period, including an open peat fire with a daub and wattle canopy and selection of traditional patchwork quilts, the Centre has exhibits about the President, his local family and general emigration history.

It was in the rear garden that the elite 1st battalion unit was formed in June 1942 and the US Ranger Centre is a tribute to them.

Andrew Jackson Centre,
Bonneybefore, Carrickfergus.

Thatchers working on
Andrew Jackson Centre
outside the US Rangers
Centre.

LARNE

Larne is a major port and has been for over 1,000 years. During the eighteenth century many Irish emigrated to America from Larne and a monument in Smiley Park commemorates the *Friends Goodwill*, the first emigrant ship to sail from Larne in May 1717 heading for Boston.

BELFAST

Primarily a Victorian creation, Belfast does have some older history. It was in Belfast Lough, in 1778, that privateer John Paul Jones, the father of the United States navy and first to fly the stars and stripes flag, victoriously fought with the English 20-gun, sloop-of-war HMS *Drake*.

Outside the city, Downhill Palace is now a ruin but will stay a solid memory for the US WWII veteran troops who were stationed here.

Belfast is the birthplace of the *Titanic*. Her keel was laid down in the Harland and Wolff shipyard in 1909 and her sea trials were on Belfast Lough before sailing away to waving city crowds in 1912. There is a memorial to the tragic liner in the gardens of Belfast City Hall which was being constructed as the dreams of the new trans-Atlantic steamers were being conceived. There are also local tributes to the ship's surgeon and the designer who chose to go down with the ship.

CRUMLIN

Lying to the south of Antrim near to the Belfast International Airport, the Ulster Aviation Centre is a former US air base with exhibits of the Wildcat, Sea Hawk, Buccaneer and amphibian Sea Hawker.

ROSTREVOR

This is a chance to wave a flag of a different stripe – or throw a few rotten eggs. Rostrevor, where the Mourne Mountains sweep down to the sea, is the birthplace of Major-General Robert Ross who captured Washington and torched the White House in 1814 during the Anglo-American war. A 100-foot obelisk along the coast road to

Warrenpoint gazes out to sea with a skirt of Victorian villas, now mostly guesthouses, at his feet.

ARMAGH

Confederate General Stonewall Jackson's ancestral site is at Waugh's Farm, The Birches in Armagh. The family also had connections to Coleraine. He was the descendant of an Ulsterman sent to America as an indentured labourer after stealing £170 while he was in London and his wife, who had lifted silver, jewellery and fine lace, who he met on board the prison ship transporting them to the New World in 1749.

BALLYGAWLEY

In 1738 a young man of 22 packed his bags and left Dergenagh near Ballygawley to set sail for Pennsylvania. His great-grandson, Ulysees S. Grant, was to become the 18th US President, 1869–77. The victorious commander of the Union Army during the American Civil War, Grant visited the land of his Ulster fathers in 1878 – although the Grant Ancestral Home is actually the farmhouse of his maternal ancestors. With mud floors and furnishings from the period, the restored two-room thatched cottage is best known for its display of traditional rural life with agricultural implements including ploughs, turf creels and a horse-drawn cart. An exhibition covers the Grant story.

There is a strong theme of the long-time neighbourly handshake across the very large pond called the Atlantic. And to honour the relationship ten new shirts were presented to incoming presidents from the linen industry for many generations. Ulster was the first stop for Amelia Earhart on the first solo women's flight across the Atlantic in 1932. And Richard Branson's balloon touched down here fifty-five years later.

Titanic Memorial, Belfast.

CHAPTER 7

The Fermanagh Waterland

Enniskillen.

Fermanagh is a magical wetland place of lakes and bogs, holy wells and cures. A third of this area of enchanted landscape and woodland is under water. Early monks moved through this watery wonderland in skin-covered boats or curraghs. Over a thousand years ago hermits and holy men stole away from the dominant Druids for a reclusive, austere life of peace and prayer on lakeland islands. And later, stately homes spread their demesnes across the lands, across the waters.

ENNISKILLEN

Wedged between Upper and Lower Lough Erne, Enniskillen town is really an island with a network of medieval lanes. The main street is broken into six arbitrary sections, each with its own name but no visible clue to the road changing in any way. Narrow alleys lead to the river between houses which may be two storeys on the landside yet six or seven storeys on the river side, so steep is its slope.

A sleepy town, the streets swell with schoolboys as the Portora Royal School ends its day of study. Founded by Royal Charter in 1608 by James I, the ruins of Portora Castle are in the grounds with its collapse reputed to be the result of errant schoolboys playing with gunpowder. This seventeenth-century academy claims both Oscar Wilde and Samuel Beckett as alumni and other old boys include the composer of *Abide With Me* as well as the importer of the first kangaroo to England in 1787. As the light fades the town closes with the only activity focussing on Blake's of the Hollow. One of Ireland's classic pubs that has been in the same family since 1887, the dark wood front bar has been untouched for 120 years.

And standing guard over his old garrison town is General G. Lowry Cole in full

Blakes of the Hollow.

eighteenth century military uniform atop a tall, fluted column. Tramp up the 108 steps for stunning views from the monument. The local born hero was raised at Florence Court, a three-storey, Palladian mansion and seat of the earls of Enniskillen and renown for the ancient yew in its grounds.

Another classic Irish house in the neighbourhood is Castle Coole designed by James Wyatt in the eighteenth century with an opulent Regency interior. Built to impress, the majestic grandeur of the Portland stone and neo-classical symmetry were created as a summer house! Step from under the ionic portico of the wide-winged mansion into the hayfields and wooded landscape beyond.

In contrast, Castle Caldwell is a romantic ruin with woodland walks. At the gate is a tribute to a local fiddler who drowned while entertaining the family on a pleasure barge:

> *On firm land only exercise your skill*
> *That you may play and drink your fill*

Cole Monument.

This was the home of the founder of nearby Belleek Pottery, Ireland's oldest pottery still making parian porcelain that is considered a prized element of a young bride's dowry around the world.

Crom Castle is a mix of lakeshore ruins that are open to the public and the nineteenth-century castle which is private, although the west wing is available for holiday rentals, which is still lived in by the descendants of the original builders. More ruins can be explored at Tully Castle, not really a castle more a fortified house from 1619 burned and abandoned after the 1641 rebellion. And Monea Castle is an intriguing ruin with crumbling Scottish-style turrets in the corners, massive towers and a dovecote.

KILLADEAS

On the banks of Lower Lough Erne, to the north of Enniskillen, is Killadeas village, home to the yellow parish church. In the graveyard of the little church stands the

Lower Lough Erne.

Killadeas church with phallic pillar.

Bishop's Stone, Killadeas church.

Celtic cross carved onto grave stone, Killadeas.

Bishop's Stone, a striking and haunting example of an early Christian carved stone from the seventh or eighth century. On one side is the troubled, open-mouth moonface of a pagan figure. And on the other side is the Christian monk or bishop touting the symbolic bell and crozier.

Wandering the graveyard there are other old stones to discover with curious carvings and Celtic crosses thought to date from this early period. A cluster gather around a pillar considered to be a pagan phallus.

Explore the wooded lakeshore at Castle Archdale Country Park. The 1773 manor house, that gives the park its name has gone and only the courtyard buildings remain including a fine eighteenth-century stable block. There is a fitting tribute to the Second World War as it was from here that the flying boats left to protect convoys from U-boat attack in the North Atlantic during WWII. And it is from the marina here that boats cross to the once holy islands that lie safely and serenely in the lough.

WHITE ISLAND

The monastic origins of White Island have largely been forgotten, being destroyed by the Vikings in 837 and are shrouded in mystery. The ruins of an ancient church stand over the old monastic site. The builders of this later Hiberno-Romanesque Church had no interest in the former site using many of the old stones in the construction. It has a stunning, curving intact doorway with arching worked shafts.

But the island is best known for its enigmatic carved figures standing along the north wall of the church. Although Christian in image the carving style is pagan. Sockets in the top of the head suggest they might have supported elements of a former wooden church. They have been gathered from around the island and lumped together in a line like they are waiting in a bus queue and it is unknown how they were used.

First up is Sheelagh-na-gig, a lewd and gleefully grinning naked female, hands on thighs. Sheelas were magical creatures often found over church doorways and windows and whether they are a celebration of fertility or a warning against lust and sins of the flesh is unknown. Next to her is a seated figure presumed to represent Christ as it is similar to an image in *The Book of Kells.* Third up is a hooded high-ranking cleric with crook and bell. Fourth in line is a figure pointing to his mouth holding a scroll who may be David in his role as psalmist. Next comes a figure with a mythical griffin-like creature followed by a fighting figure with sword, shield and a penannular brooch, an emblematic circular

Celtic ornamental clasp with attached long pin from the ninth or tenth century. The last figure wears a frown.

DEVENISH ISLAND

Across the silvery waters, windswept Devenish Island is speckled with holy buildings originating from the monastery founded by St Molaise in the sixth century during the flowering on the monasteries, although most structures date to the twelfth century.

Round tower and church, Devenish Island.

The most spectacular is a slender, high round tower soaring some 82 feet (25m) above the ground with carefully dressed curving stones. The round-headed door is about nine feet above the ground with entry being by a retractable ladder. Inside are five floors above an unlit basement. Each floor is illuminated by a single window except for the very top floor which has four windows, each with a carved face above it. Built in the late ninth or early tenth century during the time of the Viking raids the tower served as a lookout watchtower with uninterrupted views up the lough so monks could see approaching strangers. Hand bells rung as warning of possible menace or danger. It was also a store for books and treasure and a safe place for people. And this fine example is a famous symbol of Christianity in Ireland.

Devenish Island was the monastic capital of its day and the ground plan of the monks' living and praying spaces are clearly visible and early ruins include St Molaise's Oratory. On the higher ground is St Mary's Priory, a later ecclesiastical structure constructed in the fifteenth century, with a graveyard and High Cross. With a devastating fire in 1157 and the Dissolution of the Monasteries in the sixteenth century, the island's religious significance faded. But for many years after the vitality of the church buildings had waned the island continued to be favoured as a neutral assembly place for parleys and meetings between disputing clans.

BOA ISLAND

Although an island, Boa is connected to land on both sides by bridges at the northern perimeter of the lough. Down a farm lane and across a field is the overgrown Caldragh Cemetery, a graveyard dating back to early Christian times.

Quietly, among the grasses is a small inscrutable carved stone statue with big eyes and lolling tongue. This simple, mysterious character is known as a Janus figure because it has two large, pointed oval-shaped faces, one carved on each side, looking in opposite directions and with an interlace design of hair on the ajoining sides. But this is not the two-headed Roman god Janus. Part god, part man the Bronze Age carving has a hollow on top which is now a wishing nook with coins and trinkets placed there for good luck but may have been a vessel for sacrificial blood. It is considered to possibly be a Celtic god as the Celts honoured the head as the repository of the spirit after death and severed heads were symbols of triumph in battle. The Boa figure has no neck with a square torso sitting on a recently discovered base plinth with the crossed arms ending in two hands with elongated fingers.

Opposite:
Across the lough from Boa Island.

114

The figure may be a goddess rather than a god as this is the land of Badhbh, the goddess of war and a good friend to have in battle. The bilateral figure is in its original place but is joined by a smaller hunched carving known as the Badhbh figure moved from nearby Lusty Beg Island. Although less visually remarkable, this is thought to be the older stone with the Sheelagh-na-gig signature hands. It is assumed these are pagan sculptures but could come from very early Christian times when the old beliefs were intertwined with the new faith during death and burial rituals.

The loughs house many magical ancient sites. To appreciate the landscape take the stiff 700 feet ascent of 365 steps up Magho Cliffs with the reward of fresh water from a stone-arched well at the top. Upper Lough Erne which is south or below Enniskillen is dotted with ancient artificial island crannogs.

Gallon Island, close to Newtownbutler, has two weathered High Crosses one showing the New Testament, the other the Old, and gravestones with sand timers, skull and crossbones and other interesting eighteenth-century elements. At Inishmacsaint, a sixth-century monastic site founded by St Ninnid, is a plain, tenth-century cross. Tall, thin and plank-like, the two stones are joined at the head with a mortice and tenon joint and legend says it turns three times on Easter Sunday.

DRUMSKINNY

Firmly back on land there are many Neolithic sites ashore. Northeast of Lower Lough Erne is a superior megalithic mini-complex called Drumskinny created 2,000BC at the peak of the stone circle era. This miniaturised stone circle with thirty-nine close-set stones, 43 feet (13m) in diameter, with kerbed cairn and twenty-three elements and a fifteen-metre-long stone row has a vital tranquillity in its completeness nestled among trees and fields of the high bogland. There is no evidence of burial in the circle but a crude hollow-scraper and worked flints were excavated. Probably used for religious practise it is, today, considered that stone circles were for astronomical observation and functioned as calendars. It had the later reputation as a place for parley among rival clans.

The charming, concise, compact size of Drumskinny makes the place comprehensible and pleasant rather than amazing and awe inspiring. This is a cultural handshake over millennia. And for many, these ancient sites are alive through the elements and tales that thread through to modern life.

To Drumskinny Stone Circle.

Drumskinny Stone Circle.

Drumskinny Stone Circle.

The folks at the Aughakillymaude Mummers Centre at Knockninny have vibrantly embraced rural pagan rituals with traditional masked mumming performances. Aughakillymaude is the name of the small village where the troop is based and means "wooded field of the dog." The sixteen member troop perform mid-winter folk dramas based on life, death and rebirth bringing mayhem in their wake and bestowing good luck on all. Based in the restored Victorian stone village school house, their giant straw masks that are the foundation for the identity-hiding costumes are on display. Visitors can learn straw crafts from making fertility corn dollies to traditional love knots with rye and corn straw.

Right: *Drumskinny Stone Circle.*

Below: *Drumskinny Stone Circle with stone row.*

CHAPTER 8

Garden Lands of Armagh

In the north of Armagh are apple orchards and dry stone walls surrounding the fields, small in size due to the Gaelic inheritance tradition of dividing land between all family members. To the south are the drumlins, smooth rolling hills, and wild moorland.

And in the centre is the dignified city of Armagh with Georgian mansions and tree-lined malls and an eighteenth-century Observatory with dioramas. It is known as the ecclesiastical capital being the seat of both Catholic and Church of Ireland archbishops. Every October a theatre and music festival is held in the Georgian Old Bishop's Palace.

Apple orchards of Armagh.

Apple orchards of Armagh.

St Patrick founded his church here in the fifth century. Now two cathedrals, both called St Patrick's, face each other from neighbouring hilltops. Work started on St Patrick's Catholic Cathedral in 1840 but construction was suspended due to the great famine and it was not consecrated until 1904. The hats of its past dead cardinals hang around the altar. The protestant Saint Patrick's Church of Ireland Cathedral is the last of eighteen churches built in the past 1500 years on the site of an old ring fort and has the remains of King Brian Boru who defeated the Vikings in 1014.

Armagh is the second primary area of the Saint Patrick's Trail that winds down through County Down passing by Bagenal's Castle, ruined site of a Cistercian abbey founded in 1157 with a twelfth-century Celtic cross carved in granite, in Newry. If St Patrick did everything reported in legend and went everywhere that bears his name, he was a very busy man. However, the Saint Patrick Trail is anchored on fifteen sites that are actually historically related to his life, teachings and heritage, each of which can give information about other local places associated with the saint whether by fact or fable.

With prominent road signage, the trail continues to the Armagh Museum with many archaeological finds from the early Christian era, and then on to the Armagh Public Library with an ecclesiastical collection from the seventeenth and eighteenth centuries. The hands-on exhibition at Saint Patrick's Trian uses touch-screen computers to explore the life of the saint through the *Book of Armagh*, a treasured manuscript written in 807 by scribe Ferdomnach.

It is a land of prosperous farmers and violent political opinion. Come Sundays in summer expect road closures on country roads for games of bullet. The bullet is an iron ball weighing some 28oz (795g) and the game is road bowls. Players walk past silent mills, cross bridges over old trout streams closing the road while throws and a complex scoring system establish winners and losers and places in a hierarchical championship which culminates every year in early August with the All Ireland Intermediate Road Bowls Festival.

Stretching to the west, through Augher and onto Fivemiletown, is the stomping ground of the Clogher Historical Society that for decades has dug up burial chambers, dolmens and graveyards exploring everything of historical interest from presbyteries to attics. Their finds are reported the *The Clogher Record* journal.

And there is a lot to uncover. Enjoy tea and trinkets at the Clogher Valley Railway Station in Augher; the train has not run for 60 years but there is lots of memorabilia. Clamber up to Breckenridge's Folly, a prominent mausoleum built by a local squire who wanted the aristocracy that ignored him in life to see him in death every time they went to church. A hike up the damp, wooded trail to Pinnacle Peak leads to a fern and mossy area reputed to be an old Druid centre, although there is no archaeological evidence to support the theory. But there is a very large throne-like stone called St Patrick's Chair. Nearby is St Brigit's Well with a bullaun depression and reputed to never run dry and invested with magical healing powers. In between are two rag trees adorned with strips of cloth, prayers for health.

KNOCKMANY

It is a wonderful uphill walk to the Knockmany chambered cairn sitting on an escarpment commanding superb views over Clogher Valley. The tomb is linked to Aine, one of the most ancient goddesses of Ireland and has become known as Anny's Grave.

Opposite: *Clougher Valley.*

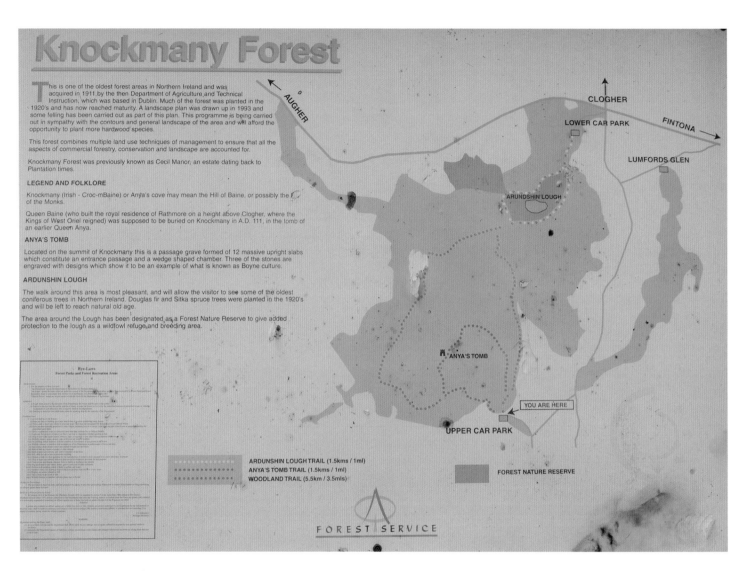

Knockmany Forest

This is one of the oldest forest areas in Northern Ireland and was acquired in 1911 by the then Department of Agriculture and Technical Instruction, which was based in Dublin. Much of the forest was planted in the 1920's and has now reached maturity. A landscape plan was drawn up in 1993 and some felling has been carried out as part of this plan. This programme is being carried out in sympathy with the contours and general landscape of the area and will afford the opportunity to plant more hardwood species.

This forest combines multiple land use techniques of management to ensure that all the aspects of commercial forestry, conservation and landscape are accounted for.

Knockmany Forest was previously known as Cecil Manor, an estate dating back to Plantation times.

LEGEND AND FOLKLORE

Knockmany (Irish - Croc-mBaine) or Anya's cove may mean the Hill of Baine, or possibly the Hill of the Monks.

Queen Baine (who built the royal residence of Rathmore on a height above Clogher, where the Kings of West Oriel reigned) was supposed to be buried on Knockmany in A.D. 111, in the tomb of an earlier Queen Anya.

ANYA'S TOMB

Located on the summit of Knockmany this is a passage grave formed of 12 massive upright slabs which constitute an entrance passage and a wedge shaped chamber. Three of the stones are engraved with designs which show it to be an example of what is known as Boyne culture.

ARDUNSHIN LOUGH

The walk around this area is most pleasant, and will allow the visitor to see some of the oldest coniferous trees in Northern Ireland. Douglas fir and Sitka spruce trees were planted in the 1920's and will be left to reach natural old age.

The area around the Lough has been designated as a Forest Nature Reserve to give added protection to the lough as a wildfowl refuge and breeding area.

AUGHER

CLOGHER

FINTONA

LOWER CAR PARK

LUMFORDS GLEN

ARUNDSHIN LOUGH

ANYA'S TOMB

YOU ARE HERE

UPPER CAR PARK

ARDUNSHIN LOUGH TRAIL (1.5kms / 1ml)
ANYA'S TOMB TRAIL (1.5kms / 1ml)
WOODLAND TRAIL (5.5km / 3.5mls)

FOREST NATURE RESERVE

FOREST SERVICE

Knockmany Forest trails.

Knockmany trail signs.

Knockmany chambered tomb stones.

Although the passage of this classic passage tomb is absent, the stones forming the chamber stand tooth-like, big and strong, an open mouth to swallow the dead into the belly of the earth. They are decorated with the best examples of tomb art in the north with circles, swirls and zig zags. Excavation shows that a stone cairn capped with earth within a stone revetment originally covered the burial chamber, which lies off centre within the cairn.

The passage grave is affectionately mentioned in *The Legend of Knockmany* by local novelist William Carleton writing in the early 1800s. But the wild cairn he would have visited has been tamed and housed, since 1959, in a concrete structure to protect the ancient stones from weather and vandalism. Should Knockmany be covered or not? Should ancient sites be signposted (most are not well signed and confusing to find) with gravel paths and car parks or left to the exploring adventurer? There is current debate in the travel, history and cultural worlds about access versus ambiance in Northern Ireland.

Knockmany chambered tomb in protective concrete housing.

HISTORIC HOUSES AND MORE

The great protector of historic sites in Northern Ireland is the National Trust that guards tracts of seashore, preserving small sites and heritage centres, as well as the big houses and stately homes. Locally these include Andress House, a seventeenth-century gentleman farmer's residence with ornate eighteenth-century plasterwork inside and a traditional farmyard with live animals and a collection of working farm tools and machinery.

Tynan Abbey was a romantic-gothic country house built at the end of the eighteenth century but bombed in 1981 with the ruins being cleared in 1998. Although there is no evidence of a religious abbey in the area, there are Celtic crosses on the site including an interesting 13 feet (4m) sculptured stone cross from the tenth century.

Charlemont Fort was similarly burned to the ground by arsonists in 1920. A star-shaped fort, the castle was constructed by Lord Mountjoy in 1602 to guard the crossing of the Blackwater River where a charming eighteenth-century cut-stone bridge still stands.

Moneypenny's Lockhouse has been spared a ruinous fate. The last lockkeeper packed his bags and left the whitewashed eighteenth-century home to rot in 2007. Now the house along with stables and bothy have been fully restored and are reached by a very pleasant, two-mile walk along the fruit-tree lined Newry Canal towpath from Portadown's Sullivan Quay car park.

But the old police station at Dungannon takes the cake for strange. The dramatic, turreted castle-like fortification is not so much a reflection on the ferocity of local criminals but more a bureaucratic mix-up. Some government clerk from the days of the Raj had muddled the plans and this building should have been a fort guarding the Khyber Pass in Afghanistan!

BEAGHMORE STONE CIRCLES

Stone circles cluster around Dunnamore, enveloped in blanket-peat bogs. And it was peat cutters in the 1940s that unearthed the impressive Beaghmore Stone Circles. Striding across the bare landscape are seven circles, six in irregular-shaped pairs and an odd one out, with over 800 small upright stones known as Dragon's Teeth, plus ten stone rows and a dozen burial mounds. The monument has some two metres of peat cut away so it can be seen, but it is not a tall structure.

The true purpose of this lonely and intricate site cannot be known. Probably a socio-religious focal point, it is considered to be a sophisticated celestial alignment constructed in relation to the movements of sun, moon and stars. Three of the stone circles point to a solstice sunrise and another is aligned to moonrise at the same time. The twelve kerbed cairns showed signs of cremation burials. The irregular formation of the circles suggests a megalithic geometry based on a 2.27 feet standard. Excavation has unearthed vessels, axes, flint implements and flakes with earlier walled field systems revealing Neolithic activity dating back to around 3,300BC as well as late Bronze Age finds from 1,535–775BC.

NAVAN FORT

Navan Fort is the Anglicized name for this great mound carpeted with a velvety fur of grass, site of an ancient hill fort. But its Gaelic name is Emain Macha, the birthplace of the twins. The mythic Queen Macha had twins, one bestowing blessings, the other curses. And she is known as the creator of this place, possibly a Celtic temple, renowned as the ceremonial crowning centre of the sovereigns of Ulster 340BC–332AD.

Navan Fort.

Navan Fort exhibition centre.

Surrounded by mystery and myths, Navan Fort lays claim to being the site of St Patrick's first stone church. It was a church centre until the Vikings arrived during the ninth and tenth centuries. A legendary archaeological treasure, there is not a lot to see at the site but a magnificently sympathetic, grass-roofed, living history visitor centre interprets the past of Ulster's Camelot with Cuchalainn as the heroic king and Deidre the beloved with a backdrop of antagonistic Druids.

In 5,000BC the sixteen-acre enclosure was defended by a massive earth mound. The ceremonial and spiritual capital of Ulster it was the centre of pagan power and culture for the Bronze Age aristocracy and Neolithic farmers. A stronghold of the Celtic kings and culture from 700BC there is evidence that in 94BC a huge timber building, possibly a temple, was erected over the cairn then ritualistically burned. A sacred site with over 7,500 years of activity, the earthwork enclosure is almost perfectly circular with a massive bank and ditch and a high mound in the centre.

The smooth mound we stand on today had a series of nine large roundhouses with political-religious ceremonial significance. A religious centre from Neolithic times it reached its peak 3,000 years later during the Iron Age just a few hundred years before Christ. It was the seat of ancient kings; the safety of the hilltop rath protected the chieftain, his liege and cattlemen and served as a giant stockade for stock. Nearby man-

Opposite: *Navan Fort.*

made ponds appear to be portals into the "otherworld" where treasure as well as animals and people were cast.

LOUGH NEAGH

The northern reaches of this orchard garden land are bordered by Lough Neagh, the largest inland sheet of water in Britain, some 150 square miles (388 sq km), with two major islands and a ferry service. Its eastern shore is kissing close to Belfast, to the north it stretches to Antrim overlooked by Shane's Castle, the ruinous stronghold and family seat the O'Neills of Clandeboy.

Its western hinterland hosts Springhill, a seventeenth-century manor house, and many Neolithic and Christian monuments which are interpreted at the An Creagan Heritage and Culture Centre. On the lakeshore is the iconic Ardboe Cross. Standing some eighteen feet high and over three feet at its widest, this tenth-century High Cross, the first of its kind in Ulster, has twenty-two carvings of biblical scenes from Adam and Eve and

Travellers and sheep share the roads in this agricultural area.

A horse grazes with the patchwork of small fields beyond.

the Old Testament on one side to the Last Judgment and the New Testament on the other. Worn by wind and rain this ringed sandstone cross and sermon stone is the remnant of a monastic settlement founded by St Coleman in 590. There are also the ruins of a sixteenth-century cross and tradition has it that before interment a coffin should be carried around it, encircling the cross. Having stood on this site for over 1,000 years the cross is in remarkable condition especially as emigrants had a habit of chipping off a flake and taking it with them to the new lands for luck.

There are two islands in the lough. Local fisherman gracing the shores, whiling away an hour or two and netting their family's tea, have a tale or two to share and tell of the islands being aristocratic bolt holes for illicit trysts. Rams Island has the remnant of a monastic round tower. And Coney Island has the ruins of a Norman motte and bailey castle and an overgrown holy well. Although inhabited since Mesolithic times, some 8,000 years BC, Coney Island was the western edge of Norman occupation in the twelfth century. Although lacking the glamour of the fairground rides of Coney Island in New York, this Coney Island has a St Patrick's Chair, Coney Cottage and the O'Neills' Tower to explore for excitement.

Cures are big in this part of the world from the fairy wishing tree with waterside amber pebbles laid on the ground at the Cranfield's holy well by the top of the lough to a contemporary healing centre at Wishing Bay on the south shore.

Such is the lure of Lough Neagh that every spring some twenty million eels, taking three years to swim across the Atlantic from the Sargasso Sea, swim up the River Bann to the lough. The eels have been a food source since the early hunter-gatherer fishermen. And until recent times fishermen used traditional hazel wood traps called skeaghs which would have been familiar to the original inhabitants.

Now the old eel fishing techniques have gone and a cooperative, set up by a local priest in defiance of purchase attempts from the international fishing industry, supplies the European market. Almost all the eels are sold outside of Ireland. Some make their way to Billingsgate, the fish market in London, but the majority go to the Netherlands and Germany where they are smoked.

But the old fishing superstitions remain. It is unlucky to have salt, whistling or a woman on board a fishing boat. It is bad luck to turn back once setting out for the lough but good luck to tie a prayer rag to the net. And you have to join a red head for three steps for good fortune if encountering a Titian-haired person on the path to the lough.

An Creagan Dolmen.

Ireland's Nobel Laureate poet Seamus Heaney was born and raised in this area of rushy fields and peat bogs writes of "the slime and silver of the fattened eel." He dedicated his 1969 collection of poems *A Lough Neagh Sequence* to "the fishermen", writing about the eels and the setting and lifting of the fishermen. The old fishing ways of the early twentieth century also inspired local poets John Colemen and Owen Toal.

Distance: This Bog walk is 3.2 miles but is chosen from a selection of hikes ranging from six miles to short walks.

Difficulty: Easy, paths through woodland and bogs are hard surfaced wooden trackways, stout shoes suggested but passable for wheelchairs in dryer weather.

Start at Peatlands Park off junction 13 on the M1. Follow the Bog Walk signs through the open tawny shades of 8,000-year-old peat land of Mullenakill Nature Reserve. Continue to Derryhubbert Bog with herons fishing in the watery ditches. Skirting the Annagarriff woodland the path zigzags to the turf cutting displays and onto the bog garden with carnivorous plants. Return to the car park past displays on the healing and domestic uses of moss.

Peatland Bog Walk.

CHAPTER 9

The Wilds of the Mourne Mountains

Northern Ireland was politically separated from the south by the Government of Ireland Act of 1922. But geology has kept the two areas apart for aeons with a chain of domed hills and lakes known as the drumlins. The Belfast-born creator of the Narnia stories, C.S. Lewis, called them "earth covered potatoes" and they are a rambler's delight.

Some few thousand years ago this natural geographical defence was built up at the weaker points. Legend has it that the Black Pig of Ulster ploughed a deep furrow with his snout to create this natural frontier. And along its path there are mounds and moats honouring the mythic pig such as Black Pig's Dyke and Black Pig's Race. Sections of this tribal boundary, an earthy Hadrian's Wall, have many curious names such as Dorsey or the Worm's Ditch.

During The Troubles crossings to the south and the Republic of Ireland were limited but roads have been open with the Single Market of 1994.

Hard on the border by Jonesborough is one of the earliest Christian monuments, the inscribed Kilnasaggart Pillar. This carved eighth-century stone stands on the ancient Tara road and has over a dozen crosses cut into the face. The stone was bequeathed by Temoc who died in 714 and excavations revealed early Christian graves radiating out from the pillar and facing the rising sun. Nearby is Moyry Castle, a three-storey ruined tower from the Elizabethan wars.

The Mourne Mountains.

MOURNE MOUNTAINS

Like flounced petticoats, hills roll down and away from Slieve Donard, 2,786 feet (850m) high, the highest of some forty-eight peaks, that are the purple heather haze of the Mourne Mountains. Peaceful and sparsely populated, this is a land of myth and magic covered with a web of tracks through bogs and fields alongside a network of grey dry-stone walls, a patchwork quilt of granite and green.

HILLTOWN

Hilltown is the small settlement in the heart of the Mournes. Hot hikers can quench their thirst at any one of the eight pubs lining the main street, a legacy from eighteenth-century smugglers who used the watering holes to divide up contraband of wine, silks and spices.

Mourne Mountains.

Church at Hilltown.

A few miles out of town on the road to Castlewellan is the Goward Dolmen also called Cloughmore Cromlech, a chieftain's portal grave. Nestled in a farmer's field, this huge megalithic dolmen has a 50 ton granite capstone which has slithered off the three massive uprights that once housed a double burial. Bones and pottery from the Neolithic period were unearthed here during excavations.

ROSTREVOR

Rostrevor is the southern gateway to the Mourne Mountains. Victorian frontages line the coastal towns of Rostrevor and Warrenpoint which lie in the shadow of Slievemartin.

Staring out to sea along the coast to Warrenpoint is the 100 feet tall granite obelisk commemorating local son Major-General Robert Ross, he whose claim to fame is torching the White House in Washington in 1814.

Terrace Houses, Rostrevor.

Past Warrenpoint, Narrow Water Castle is a tower house fortification on a strategic spur of rock jutting out into the estuary. Built in the 1560s on the site of an earlier keep the tower was home to the English garrison and its battlements, murder hole and bawn wall stand firm today in an atmospheric watery spot.

KILKEEL COAST

The smell of fish wafting over Kilkeel as one heads down to the harbour is a clue to the importance this port has for the fishing fleet. Winding streets lead back up to the ruins of a fourteenth-century church and fort. Kilkeel takes its name from the old church as it derives from the Gaelic Cill Chaoil meaning "church in a narrow place."

Constructed in 1388 and dedicated to St Colman del Mourne, the church was important in the middle ages although Kilkeel has been a Christian settlement since the eleventh century. The attached graveyard was in use through 1916 and the last burials were victims of an infamous and tragic collision between two steamer ships in Carlingford Lough. Kilkeel was the capital of the ancient Kingdom of Mourne and is an entry into the Mournes through the Silent Valley. A dolmen lies to the northeast of town.

Along the coast is the small picturesque seaside town of Annalong with little boats bobbing in the harbour, nets being repaired onshore and a working corn mill inland. The Annalong Cornmill was built in the early 1800s and operated through the 1960s, one of the last working watermills in Ulster. As the mill was being built the harbour was enlarged to receive schooners with granite cargo. Besides pleasure craft, current working fishing is focussed on creeling for lobsters and the pots are piled up on the quayside.

Visitors can see demonstrations of wheat and oat grinding on three pairs of mill stones as the mill's building still retains much of the original machinery including the 15 foot waterwheel and grain drying kiln. Farmers brought their harvested grain to be ground and if cash was short the miller would be paid in kind bartering the work for a bag of oats.

NEWCASTLE

On the ocean side skirt of Slieve Donard, the king of the Mournes at 2796 feet (852m), Newcastle is dusted with the Edwardian charm of its turn of the century heyday and is the starting point for many walks among the peaks, most begin at Donard Park. The hotel bearing the peak's name hosted Charlie Chaplin in 1921 and his signature is on display. He stayed here while divorcing his wife only to receive the news that his true love, Hetty Kelly, had died.

WALKING IN THE MOURNE MOUNTAINS

At every turn there is an ancient track or modern footpath to wander or hike the entire Mourne area. At the foot of Slieve Donard, Newcastle is the launch pad for hill walking, pony treks and scenic drives in the Mournes and country rambles through neighbouring Tollymore Forest Park. Maps are essential as paths are not always clearly marked. The weather can change for the better or worse in a second so be prepared.

A gentle walk runs 4 miles (6km) runs along the Mourne Coastal Path along a rocky shoreline from Bloody Bridge, site of a massacre in the 1641 Rebellion, to Dunmore

Head. Serious hill walkers head inland for the Hill Walk covering the five main peaks leaving the coast for Hilltown along the Brandy Pad smuggler's track and exploring the Mournes along the Trassey Track, the granite quarrymen's path. The Granite Trail heads out from Newcastle; now peaceful this old "Bogie" track once resounded to the echo of hammer and anvil as granite was mined to pave the burgeoning cities of Belfast, Liverpool and London. Well-paved paths make walking easy, especially with a push or wheel chair, along the scenic trails at Slieve Gullion Forest Park and along fourteen locks of the Newry Canal, completed in 1742, which heads out of Newry for twenty miles of towpath towards Portadown.

The Mourne Mountains.

WALK I

Distance: 12 miles.

Allow: 6 Hours.

Difficulty: Hard, climbing and tracks.

Map essential OS ref 373304 sheet 29.

Following the clear water of the Glen River the woodland fades and a gravel path runs towards the Great Mourne Wall built in 1904–22 to enclose the Silent Valley Reservoir dammed in the 1920s. Follow the wall for a steep climb to the summit of Slieve Donard, Ulster's highest peak. The Brandy Pad, an old smuggler's trail, passes below the Castles Rock Towers among the ridges with granite tors. Take a 400 feet (120m) detour to Diamond Rocks.

Continue to Hare's Gap, tramp along the Tassey River past old sheep pens. Gorse banks gather as the trail joins the Ulster Way signed path and stiles lead into the hazel coppice and through fir plantations on to Parnell's Bridge. Stay with the river bank as the Ulster Way heads south, do not cross the bridge but carry on to the small lake.

WALK 2

Distance: 4+ miles.

Difficulty: Easy to moderate some uneven, stony tracks. Stout shoes essential.

Start at the Donard Car Park near Newcastle's seafront and follow road along to Donard Bridge. Cross and take the stony path along the river through the shady gnarled oaks. Continue along the river past clear pools to the next bridge. Cross over to the right bank and stay on this side of the river through glades of twisted trunks, towering pine and slabs of rugged granite. Let your imagination run riot, this is *Narnia* country. C.S Lewis was inspired by this isolated land to create his own fairytale magical kingdom.

Climbing higher, woodland gives way to open heather moor just past the next bridge by a domed stone ice house. Ahead are three peaks called slieves and you approach the Glen River headwaters. Look out for hares known as shape shifters believed to magically take human form. Once the path crosses the stream take a break and either retrace your steps and return to the car park or make the steep scramble up Slieve Donard, the highest peak of the Mournes at 852m, which will add another couple of hours to the hike.

The Mourne Mountains.

For more information:

Mythic Ireland by Michael Dames
Stone Circles of Great Britain by Aubrey Burl
Monumental About .... series focussing on different areas
The Complete Ulster Way Walks by Paddy Dillon
Anything by William Carleton especially *The Black Prophet* (1847) or *Legend of Knockmany.*
Skywatchers, Shamans and Kings by E.C. Krupp
The Stars and the Stones: Ancient Art and Astronomy in Ireland by Martin Brenan
Early Ireland by Michael O'Kelly

www.megalithics.com/ireland
www.follies-trust.org
www.IrishMegaliths.org.uk
www.familyulster.com researches family history and will arrange tours of relevant places.
www.ancestryireland.com promotes interest in history and genealogy in Ulster.
Ulster Archaeological Society www.uarcsoc.org
www. nationaltrust.org.uk
www.translink.co.uk: for public transport information.

Thanks to:
Hastings Hotels and all the staff at Ballygally Castle.
Stenaline Ferries
Bushmills Distillery
All the many helpful staff at the tourist boards and information centres across the region especially the exceptional Fiona Ure in Belfast and Valentina Nixon in Fermanagh.
Judy Crawford
And also to the creative hand of Sonora Dicker